The Tanner Lectures on Human Values

THE TANNER LECTURES
ON HUMAN VALUES

V

1984

Carlos Fuentes, Ilya Prigogine, David Gauthier,
Herbert A. Simon, H. C. Robbins Landon

Sterling M. McMurrin, *Editor*

UNIVERSITY OF UTAH PRESS — Salt Lake City
CAMBRIDGE UNIVERSITY PRESS — Cambridge, London, Melbourne, Sydney

Published in North and South America
and the Philippines
by the University of Utah Press,
Salt Lake City, Utah 84112, U.S.A.,
and in Great Britain and all other countries by
The Press Syndicate of the University of Cambridge
The Edinburgh Building, Shaftesbury Road,
Cambridge CB2 2RU, and
296 Beaconsfield Parade, Middle Park, Melbourne 3206
Australia.

The paper in this book meets the standards
for permanence and durability established by
the Committee on Production Guidelines for Book Longevity
of the Council on Library Resources.

THE TANNER LECTURES ON HUMAN VALUES

Appointment as a Tanner lecturer is a recognition of uncommon capabilities and outstanding scholarly or leadership achievement in the field of human values. The lecturers may be drawn from philosophy, religion, the humanities and sciences, the creative arts and learned professions, or from leadership in public or private affairs. The lectureships are international and intercultural and transcend ethnic, national, religious, or ideological distinctions.

The purpose of the Tanner Lectures is to advance and reflect upon the scholarly and scientific learning relating to human values and valuation. This purpose embraces the entire range of values pertinent to the human condition, interest, behavior, and aspiration.

The Tanner Lectures were formally founded on July 1, 1978, at Clare Hall, Cambridge University. They were established by the American scholar, industrialist, and philanthropist, Obert Clark Tanner. In creating the lectureships, Professor Tanner said, "I hope these lectures will contribute to the intellectual and moral life of mankind. I see them simply as a search for a better understanding of human behavior and human values. This understanding may be pursued for its own intrinsic worth, but it may also eventually have practical consequences for the quality of personal and social life."

Permanent Tanner lectureships, with lectures given annually, are established at six institutions: Clare Hall, Cambridge University; Harvard University; Brasenose College, Oxford University; Stanford University; the University of Michigan; and the University of Utah. Each year lectureships may be granted to not more than four additional colleges or universities for one year only. The institutions are selected by the Trustees in consultation with an Advisory Commission.

The sponsoring institutions have full autonomy in the appointment of their lecturers. A major purpose of the lecture program is the publication and wide distribution of the Lectures in an annual volume.

The Tanner Lectures on Human Values is a nonprofit corporation administered at the University of Utah under the direction of a self-perpetuating, international Board of Trustees and with the advice and counsel of an Advisory Commission. The Trustees meet annually to enact policies that will ensure the quality of the lectureships.

The entire lecture program, including the costs of administration, is fully and generously funded in perpetuity by an endowment of the University of Utah by Professor Tanner and Mrs. Grace Adams Tanner.

Obert C. Tanner was born in Farmington, Utah, in 1904. He was educated at the University of Utah, Harvard University, and Stanford University. He has served on the faculty of Stanford University and is presently Emeritus Professor of Philosophy at the University of Utah. He is the founder and chairman of the O. C. Tanner Company, manufacturing jewelers.

STERLING M. MCMURRIN
University of Utah

THE ADVISORY COMMISSION

DEREK C. BOK
President of Harvard University

HAROLD T. SHAPIRO
President of the University of Michigan

RICHARD W. LYMAN
President of Stanford University

CONTENTS

PREFACE TO VOLUME V

Since the Tanner Lectures on Human Values were established, lectures have been given at the six founding institutions: Clare Hall, Cambridge University; Harvard University; the University of Michigan; Brasenose College, Oxford University; Stanford University; and the University of Utah.

In addition, one-year lectureships have been granted to Utah State University (1978–79), Hebrew University at Jerusalem (1980–81), Australian National University (1981–82), Jawaharlal Nehru University (1982–83), and the University of Helsinki (1983–84). A 1984–85 lectureship has been established at the Queen's University of Belfast.

The Tanner lecturers have been appointed from a broad spectrum of interests and experiences. The register of lecturers includes philosophers, scientists, statesmen, historians, economists, artists, publishers — all of whom are persons of high achievement who have made and are making important contributions to the analysis and substance of social and personal values. The lecture subjects have included matters pertaining to the environment, heredity, disarmament, international and domestic politics, justice, the economy, drugs and society, music, and the literary arts. They clearly exhibit the complex and multiple character of the historical development and current structure of human values, the nature of the most crucial value problems, and the difficult tasks confronting those who must attempt the solution of those problems.

Listed in this volume are the Tanner lecturers and their subjects through the current academic year, 1983–84. This year's Lectures will be published in Volume VI, in the spring of 1985. General indices of the first five volumes have been prepared and are published here in a form that will allow their being copied to accompany earlier volumes in the series. While all the contents of the Tanner Lectures volumes are under copyright protection, the Trustees permit the photocopying of the individual indices to enhance the usefulness of the series volumes.

A Writer from Mexico

CARLOS FUENTES

THE TANNER LECTURES ON HUMAN VALUES

Delivered at
The University of Utah

May 3 and 4, 1983

CARLOS FUENTES, novelist and playwright, lived and studied in countries around the world as the son of a career diplomat and Mexican ambassador to Holland, Panama, Portugal, and Italy. He was educated at the University of Mexico and at the Institut des Hautes Etudes Internationales in Geneva. Later, as a diplomat himself, Mr. Fuentes continued his travels as secretary to the Mexican member of the United Nations International Law Commission in Geneva, as director of International Cultural Relations for Mexico's Ministry of Foreign Affairs, and eventually as Mexican ambassador to France.

Mr. Fuentes has written prolifically from a perspective of three distinct cultures, he explains—Latin American, North American, and European. His experience in New Deal America, wartime Chile and Argentina, then Mexico and Europe provided rich breeding ground for his first novels, and he also credits writers Alfonso Reyes and Octavio Paz of Mexico, Pablo Neruda of Chile, and writers of the post-war generation in Europe with providing important contributions to his own development.

I

I was born on November 11, 1928, under the sign I would have chosen anyway, Scorpio, and on a date shared with Dostoevsky, Cromelynk and Vonnegut. My mother was rushed from a steaming movie house in those days before Colonel Buendía took his son to discover ice in the tropics. She was seeing King Vidor's version of *La Bohème* with John Gilbert and Lillian Gish. Perhaps the pangs of my birth were provoked by this anomaly: a silent screen version of Puccini's opera. Since then the operatic and the cinematographic have tugged at war with my words, as if expecting that the Scorpio of fiction shall rise from silent music and from blind images.

All of this, let me add to clear up my biography, took place in the sweltering heat of Panama City, where my father was beginning his diplomatic career as an *attaché* to the Mexican Legation (in those days, Embassies were established only in the most important capitals, no place where the mean average year-round temperature was in the perpetual nineties). Since my father was a convinced Mexican nationalist, the problem of where I should be born had to be resolved under the sign, not of Scorpio, but of the Eagle and the Serpent. Yet the Mexican Legation, although it had extraterritorial rights, did not even have a territorial midwife; and the minister, a fastidious bachelor from Sinaloa called Ignacio Norris, who resembled the poet Quevedo as one pince-nez resembles another, would have none of me suddenly appearing on the Legation parquet, even if the Angel Gabriel had announced me as a future Mexican writer of some, although debatable, merit.

So if I could not be born in a fictitious, extraterritorial Mexico, neither would I be born in that even more fictitious extension of the United States of America, the Canal Zone, where the best hospitals, naturally, were. So between two territorial fictions and a mercifully silent close-up of John Gilbert, I arrived in the nick of time at the Gorgas Hospital in Panama City at eleven o'clock that night.

The problem of my baptism then arose. As if the waters of the two nearby oceans touching one another through the iron finger-tips of the Canal were not enough, I had to undergo a double cere-mony: my religious baptism took place in Panama, because my mother, a devout Roman Catholic, demanded it with as much urgency as Tristram Shandy's parents, although with less original methods. My nationalist baptism, however, took place a few months later in Mexico City, where my father, an incorrigible Jacobin and priest-eater until the end, insisted that I be registered in the civil books established by Benito Juárez. Thus, I appear as a native of Mexico City for all legal purposes, and this anomaly further illustrates a central fact of my life and my writing: I am a Mexican by will and by imagination.

All of this came to a head in the 1930's. By then, my father was counselor of the Mexican Embassy in Washington, D.C., and I grew up in the vibrant world of the American thirties, more or less between the inauguration of Citizen Roosevelt and the inter-diction of Citizen Kane. When I arrived here, Dick Tracy had just met Tess Truehart. As I left, Clark Kent was meeting Lois Lane. You are what you eat. You are also the comics you peruse as a child.

At home, my father made me read Mexican history, study Mexican geography and understand the names, the dreams and defeats of Mexico: a non-existent country, I then thought, in-vented by my father in order to nourish my infant imagination with yet another marvelous fiction: a land of Oz with a green cactus road, a landscape and a soul so different from those of the United States that they appeared as a fantasy.

A cruel fantasy: the history of Mexico was a history of crush-ing defeats, whereas I lived in a world, that of my D.C. public school, which celebrated victories, one victory after another, from Yorktown to New Orleans to Chapultepec to Appomattox to San Juan Hill to Beaulieu Wood: had this nation never known defeat? Sometimes, the names of your victories were the same as the names of Mexico's defeats and humiliations: Veracruz. Pershing. Indeed: from the Halls of Montezuma to the shores of Tripoli. In the map of my imagination, as the United States expanded westward, Mexico contracted southward. Miguel Hidalgo, the Father of Mexican independence, ended with his head exhibited on a lance at the city gates of Chihuahua. Imagine George and Martha beheaded at Mount Vernon.

To the south, sad songs, sweet nostalgia, impossible desires. To the north, self-confidence, faith in progress, boundless optimism. Mexico, the imaginary country, dreamt of a painful past; the United States, the real country, dreamt of a happy future.

The French equate intelligence with rational discourse, the Russians with intense soul-searching. For a Mexican, intelligence is inseparable from maliciousness — in this, as in many other things, we are quite Italian: *furberia*, roguish slyness, and the cult of appearances, *la bella figura*, are Italianate traits present everywhere in Latin America: Rome, more than Madrid, is our spiritual capital in this sense.

For me, as a child, the United States appeared as a world where intelligence was equated with energy, zest, enthusiasm. The North American world blinds us with its energy; we cannot see ourselves, we must see *you*. The United States is a world full of cheerleaders, prize-giving, singin' in the rain: the baton-twirler, the Oscar awards, the musical comedies cannot be repeated elsewhere; in Mexico the Hollywood statuette would come dipped in poisoned paint; in France Gene Kelly would constantly stop in his steps to reflect: *Je danse, donc je suis*.

Many things impressed themselves on me during those vibrant years of the New Deal. The United States — would you believe it? — was a country where things worked, where nothing ever broke down: trains, plumbing, roads, punctuality, personal security seemed to function perfectly, at least at the eye level of a young Mexican diplomat's son living in a residential hotel on Washington's 16th Street, facing Meridian Hill Park, where nobody was then mugged and where our superb furnished seven-room apartment cost us one hundred and ten pre-inflation dollars a month. Yes, in spite of all the problems, the livin' seemed easy during those long Tidewater summers when I became, perhaps, the first and only Mexican to prefer grits to guacamole. I also became the original Mexican Calvinist: an invisible taskmaster called Puritanical Duty shadows my every footstep: I shall not deserve anything unless I work relentlessly for it, with iron discipline, day after day. Sloth is sin, and if I do not sit at my typewriter every day at 8 A.M. for a working day of seven to eight hours, I will surely go to hell. No *siestas* for me, alas and alack and *hélas* and *ayayay*: how I came to envy my Latin brethren, unburdened by the Protestant work ethic, and why must I, to this very day, read Hermann Broch and scribble on my black notebook on a sunny Mexican beach, instead of lolling the day away and waiting for the coconuts to fall?

But the United States in the thirties went far beyond my personal experience. The nation that de Tocqueville had destined to share dominance over half the world realized that, in effect, only a continental state could be a modern state; in the thirties, the U.S.A. had to decide *what to do* with its new, world-wide power, and Franklin Roosevelt taught us to believe that the first thing was for the United States to show that it was capable of living up to its ideals. I learnt then — my first political lesson — that this is your true greatness, not, as was to be the norm in my lifetime, material wealth, not arrogant power misused against weaker peoples, not ignorant ethnocentrism burning itself out in contempt for others.

As a young Mexican growing up in your country, my primary impression was that of a nation of boundless energy, imagination, and the will to confront and solve the great social issues of the times without blinking or looking for scapegoats. It was the impression of a country identified with its own highest principles: political democracy, economic well-being and faith in its human resources, especially in that most precious of all capitals, the renewable wealth of education and research.

Franklin Roosevelt, then, restored America's self-respect in this essential way, not by macho posturing. I saw the United States in the thirties lift itself by the bootstraps from the dead dust of Oklahoma and the gray lines of the unemployed in Detroit, much as a convalescent football player springs back to the field of his greatest triumphs; and this image of health was reflected in my daily life, in my reading of Mark Twain, in the images of movies and newspapers, in the North American capacity for mixing fluffy illusion and hard-bitten truth, self-celebration and self-criticism: the madcap heiresses played by Carole Lombard coexisted with the Walker Evans photographs of hungry, old-at-thirty migratory mothers, and the nimble tread of the feet of Fred Astaire did not silence the heavy stomp of the boots of Tom Joad.

My school — a public school, non-confessional, co-educational, and racially integrated — reflected these realities and their basically egalitarian thrust. I believed in the democratic simplicity of my teachers and chums, and above all I believed I was, naturally, in a totally unself-conscious way, a part of that world. It is important, at all ages and in all occupations, to be "popular" in the United States; I have known no other society where the values of "regularity" are so highly prized. I was popular, I was "regular." Until a day in March — March the eighteenth, 1938.

On that day, a man from another world, the imaginary country of my childhood, the President of Mexico, Lázaro Cárdenas, nationalized the holdings of foreign oil companies. The headlines in the North American press denounced the "communist" government of Mexico and its "red" president; they demanded the invasion of Mexico in the sacred name of private property, and Mexicans, under international boycott, were invited to drink their oil.

Instantly, surprisingly, I became a pariah in my school. Cold shoulders, aggressive stares, epithets, and sometimes blows. Children know how to be cruel, and the cruelty of their elders is the surest residue of the malaise the young feel towards things strange, things other, things that reveal our own ignorance or insufficiency. This was not reserved for me or for Mexico: at about the same time, an extremely brilliant boy of eleven arrived from Germany. He was a Jew and his family had fled from the Nazis. I shall always remember his face, dark and trembling, his aquiline nose and deep-set, bright eyes surrounded by sadness; the sensitivity of his hands and the strangeness of it all to his American companions. This young man, Hans Berliner, was a brilliant mathematical mind and he walked and saluted like a Central European, he wore short pants and high woven stockings, Tyrolean jackets and an air of displaced courtesy that infuriated the popular, regular, feisty, knickered, provincial, depression-era little sons-of-bitches at Henry Cooke Public School on 13th Street, N.W.

The shock of alienation and the shock of recognition are sometimes one and the same. What was different made others afraid, less of what was different than of themselves, of their own incapacity to recognize themselves in the alien.

I discovered that my father's country was real. And that I belonged to it. Mexico was my identity yet I lacked it; Hans Berliner suffered more than I — headlines from Mexico are soon forgotten; another great issue becomes all-important for a wonderful ten days' media feast — yet he owned his identity as a Central European Jew. I do not know what became of him. Over the years, I have always expected to see him receive a Nobel Prize in one of the sciences. Surely, if he lived, he integrated himself into North American society. I had to look at the photographs of President Cárdenas: he was a man of another lineage; he did not appear in the repertory of glossy, seductive images of the saleable North American world. He was a mestizo, Spanish and Indian, with a faraway, green and liquid look in his eyes, as if he were trying to remember a mute and ancient past.

Was that past mine as well? Could I dream the dreams of the country suddenly revealed in a political act as something more than a demarcation of frontiers on a map or a little hill of statistics in a yearbook? I believe I then had the intuition that I would not rest until I revealed to myself that common destiny which depended upon yet another community: the community of times. The United States had made me believe that we live only for the future; Mexico, Cárdenas, the events of 1938, made me understand that only in an act of the present can we make present the past as well as the future: to be a Mexican was to identify a hunger for being, a desire for dignity rooted in many forgotten centuries and in many centuries yet to come, but rooted here, now, in the instant, in the vigilant time of Mexico I later learned to understand in the stone serpents of Teotihuacán and in the polychrome angels of Oaxaca.

Of course, as happens in childhood, all these deep musings had no proof of existence outside an act that was, more than a prank, a form of affirmation. In 1939, my father took me to see a film at the old RKO Keith in Washington. It was called *Man of Conquest* and it starred Richard Dix as Sam Houston. When Dix/Houston proclaimed the secession of the Republic of Texas from Mexico, I jumped on the theater seat and proclaimed on my own and from the full height of my nationalist ten years, "Viva México! Death to the Gringos!"

My embarrassed father hauled me out of the theater, but then his pride in me did not resist a leak about my first rebellious act to the *Washington Star*. So that I appeared for the first time in a newspaper and became a child celebrity for the acknowledged ten-day span. I read Andy Warhol *avant l'air-brush*: Everyone shall be famous for at least five minutes.

In the wake of my father's diplomatic career I travelled to Chile and fully entered the universe of the Spanish language, of

Latin American politics and its adversities. President Roosevelt had resisted tremendous pressures to apply sanctions and even invade Mexico by force to punish my country for recovering its own wealth. Likewise, he did not seek to destabilize the Chilean radicals, communists and socialists democratically elected to power in Chile under the banners of the Popular Front.

In the early forties, the vigour of Chile's political life was contagious: active unions, active parties, electoral campaigns all spoke of the political health of this, the most democratic of Latin American nations. Chile was a politically verbalized country. It was no coincidence that it was also the country of the great Spanish-American poets, Gabriela Mistral, Vicente Huidobro, Pablo Neruda.

I only came to know Neruda and became his friend many years later. This King Midas of poetry would write, in his literary testament rescued from a gutted house and a nameless tomb, a beautiful song to the Spanish language: the conquistadores, he said, took our gold, but they left us their gold: they left us our words.

Neruda's gold, I learnt in Chile, was the property of all. One afternoon on the beach at Lota in Southern Chile I saw the miners as they came out, mole-like, from their hard work many feet under the sea, extracting the coal of the Pacific Ocean. They sat around a bonfire and sang, with a guitar, a poem from Neruda's *Canto General*. I told them that the author would be thrilled to know that his poem had been set to music.

What author?, they asked me in surprise.

For them, Neruda's poetry had no author, it came from afar, it had always been sung, like Homer's. It was the poetry, as Croce said of the *Iliad*, "d'un popolo intero poetante," of an entire poetizing people. It was the document of the original identity between poetry and history.

I learnt in Chile that Spanish could be the language of free men. I was also to learn in my lifetime, precisely in Chile, the fragility of both our language and our freedom when Richard Nixon, unable to destroy American democracy, destroyed Chilean democracy and sent forth Henry Kissinger to do in Chile what Leonid Brezhnev had done in Czechoslovakia.

An anonymous language, a language that belongs to us all, as Neruda's poem belonged to those miners on the beach, yet a language that can be kidnapped, impoverished, sometimes jailed, sometimes murdered. Let me summarize this paradox: Chile offered me and the other writers of my generation in Santiago both the essential fragility of a cornered language, Spanish, and the protection of the Latin of our times, the *lingua franca* of the modern world, the English language. At The Grange School under the awesome beauty of the Andes, José Donoso and Jorge Edwards, Roberto Torreti, the late Luis Alberto Heyremans and myself, by then all budding amateurs, wrote our first exercises in literature within this mini-Britannia. We all ran strenuous cross-country races, got caned from time to time and recuperated reading Swinburne; and we received huge doses of rugby, Ruskin, porridge for breakfast, and stiff-upper-lipped reception of military defeats. But when Montgomery broke through at Alamein, the assembled school tossed caps in the air and hip-hup hurrahed to death. In South America, clubs were named after George Canning and football teams after Lord Cochrane; no matter that English help to win independence led to English economic imperialism from oil in Mexico to railways in Argentina. There was a secret thrill in our hearts: our Spanish conquerors had been beaten by the English; the defeat of Philip II's invincible Armada compensated for the crimes of Cortés, Pizarro, and Valdivia. If Britain was an empire, at least she was a democratic one.

And here lay, for my generation, the central contradiction of our relationship with the English-speaking world: you have universalized the values of modernity, freedom, economic development, and political democracy; but when in Latin America we move, in our own way, according to our own cultural tradition, to achieve them, your governments brand us as "Marxist-Leninist" tools, side with the military protectors of a status quo dating back from the Spanish Conquest, attribute the dynamics of change to a Soviet conspiracy, and finally corrupt the movement towards modernity that you yourselves have fostered.

All of this can be debated in English; it can only be created in Spanish. Rhetoric, said William Butler Yeats, is the language of our fight with others; poetry is the name of our fight with ourselves. My passage from English to Spanish decided the concrete expression of what, before, in Washington, had been the revelation of an identity. I wanted to write and I wanted to write in order to show myself that my identity and my country were real: now, in Chile, as I started to scribble my first stories and even publish them in school magazines, I learnt that I should write precisely in Spanish.

After all, the English language did not need one more writer. (I have said many times that the English language has always been alive and kicking and, if it becomes drowsy, there will always be an Irishman . . .)

In Chile I knew the possibilities of our language to give wings to freedom and poetry; the impression was enduring, it links me forever to that sad and wonderful land, it still inhabits me and it transformed me into a man who only knows how to dream, love, insult and write in Spanish. It also left me wide open to an incessant interrogation: What happened to this universal language, Spanish, which after the seventeenth century ceased to be a language of life, creation, dissatisfaction, and personal powers and became once too often a language of mourning, sterility, rhetorical applause, and abstract power? Where were the threads of my tradition, where could I, writing in the mid-twentieth century in Latin America, find the direct link to the great living presences I was then starting to read, my lost Cervantes, my old Quevedo, dead because he could not tolerate one more writer, my Góngora, abandoned in a gulf of loneliness?

At sixteen I finally went to live permanently in Mexico and found the answers to my quest for identity and language there,

written in the thin air of a plateau of stone and dust that is
the negative Indian image of another highland, that of Central
Spain.

But between Santiago and Mexico City, I spent six wonderful
months in Argentina. They were, in spite of their brevity, so important in this reading and writing of myself that I must give
them their full worth: Buenos Aires was then, as always, the most
beautiful, sophisticated and civilized city in Latin America, but
in the summer of 'forty-four, as street pavements melted under the
heat and the city smelt of cheap wartime gasoline, raw hides
emanating from the port, and chocolate *éclairs* emanating from
the *confiterías*, Argentina had seen a succession of military coups:
General Rawson had overthrown President Castillo of the cattle
oligarchy, but General Ramírez had then overthrown Rawson and
now General Farrel had overthrown Ramírez: A young colonel
called Juan Domingo Perón was General Farrel's up-and-coming
Minister of Labor and I heard an actress called Eva Duarte interpret the roles of "great women in history" on Radio Belgrano. A
stultifying hack novelist using the pen name "Hugo Wast" was
assigned the Ministry of Education under his real name of Martínez Zuviría and brought all of his anti-Semitic, un-democratic
and pro-fascist phobias to the Buenos Aires high school system,
which I had suddenly been plunked into. Coming from the America of the New Deal, the ideal of revolutionary Mexico, and the
politics of the Popular Front in Chile, I could not stomach this,
rebelled and was granted a full summer of wandering around
Buenos Aires, free for the first time in my life, following my preferred tango orchestras — Canaro, D'Arienzo, and Anibal Troilo,
alias "Pichuco" — as they played all summer long in the Renoir-
like shades and lights of the rivers and pavilions of El Tigre and
Maldonado. Now, the comics were in Spanish: Mutt and Jeff
were Benitín y Eneas. But Argentina had its own comic-book imperialism: through Billiken and Patorozú, all the children of Latin
America knew from the crib that "Las Malvinas son Argentinas."

Two very important things happened. First, I lost my virginity. We lived in this apartment building on the leafy corner of Callao and Quintana, and after 10 A.M. nobody was left there except myself, an old and deaf Polish doorkeeper, and a beautiful Czech woman, age thirty, whose husband produced films. I went up to ask her for her *Sintonía*, which was the Radio Guide of the forties, because I wanted to know when Evita was doing the life of Joan of Arc. She said that had already passed, but that the next program was the life of Madame du Barry. I wondered if Madame du Barry's life was as interesting as Joan of Arc's. She said it was certainly less saintly and, besides, it could be emulated. How?, I said innocently. The rest was my beautiful apprenticeship. We made each other very happy. And also very sad: this was not the liberty of love, but rather its libertine variety: we loved in hiding. I was too young to be a real sadist. So it had to end.

The other important thing was that I started reading Argentine literature, right from the gaucho poems to Sarmiento's *Memories of Provincial Life* to Cané's *Juvenilia* to Güiraldes' *Don Segundo Sombra* to . . . to . . . to (this was as good as discovering that Joan of Arc was also sexy) to: Borges. I have never wanted to meet Borges personally because he belongs only to that summer in B.A. He belongs to my personal discovery of Latin American literature.

II

Extremes of Latin America: if Cuba is the Andalusia of the New World, the Mexican plateau is its Castilla: parched and brown, inhabited by suspicious cats burnt too many times by foreign invasions, Mexico is the sacred zone of a secret hope: the Gods shall return.

Mexican space is closed, jealous and self-contained. In contrast, Argentinian space is open and dependent on the foreign: migrations, exports, imports, words. Mexican space was vertically sacralized thousands of years ago. Argentinian space patiently awaits its horizontal profanation.

I arrived at the Mexican highland from the Argentinian pampa when I was sixteen years old. As I said, it was better to study in a country where the minister of education was Jaime Torres Bodet than in a country where he was "Hugo Wast." This was not the only contrast, nor the most important one. A land isolated by its very nature — desert, mountain, chasm, sea, jungle, fire, ice, fugitive mists, and a sun that never blinks — Mexico is a multi-levelled temple that rises abruptly, blind to horizons, an arrow that wounds the sky but refuses the dangerous frontiers of the land, the canyons, the sierras without a human footprint, whereas the pampa is nothing if not an eternal frontier, the very portrait of the horizon, the sprawling flatland of a latent expansion awaiting, like a passive lover, the vast and rich overflow from that concentration of the transitory represented by the commercial metropolis of Buenos Aires, what Ezequiel Martínez Estrada called Goliath's head on David's body.

Mexicans descend from the Aztecs.

Argentinians descend from ships.

It is important to appreciate this distinction in order to understand the verbal differences between the Mexican culture, which, long before Paul Valéry, knew itself to be mortal, and the Argentinian culture, founded on the optimism of powerful migratory currents from Europe, innocent of sacred stones or aboriginal promises.

Mexico, closed to immigration by the TTT — that is, the Tremendous Texas Trauma that from 1836 cured us once and for all of the temptation of receiving Caucasian colonists because they had airport names like Houston and Austin and Dallas — devoted its populations to breed like rabbits: blessed by the pope, Coatlicue and Jorge Negrete, we are, all seventy million of us, Catholics in the Virgin Mary, misogynists in the stone goddesses, and *machistas* in the singing, pistol-packing, *charro*.

The pampa goes on waiting: twenty-five million Argentinians today, hardly five million more than in 1945, half of them in Buenos Aires.

Language in Mexico is ancient, old as the oldest dead. The eagles of the Indian empire fell and it suffices to read the poems of the defeated to understand the vein of sadness that runs through Mexican literature, the feeling that words are identical to farewells:

"Where shall we go to now, oh my friends?" asks the Aztec poet of the Fall of Tenochtitlan: "The smoke lifts; the fog extends. Cry, my friends. Cry, oh cry." And the contemporary poet Xavier Villaurrutia, four centuries later, again sings from the very bed of the same, but now dried-up lake, and its dry stones:

> In the midst of a silence deserted as a street before the crime
> Without even breathing so that nothing may disturb my death
> In this wall-less solitude
> When the angels fled
> In the grave of my bed I leave my bloodless statue.

A sad, underground language, forever being lost and recovered; I soon learnt that Spanish as spoken in Mexico answered to six unwritten rules:

First. Never say the familiar *tu* — thou — if you can use the formal you — *usted*.

Second. Never use the possessive pronoun in the first person, but rather in the second person, as in "This is *your* home."

Third. Always use the first person singular to refer to your own troubles, as in "Me fue del carajo, mano." But use the first-person plural when you refer to your successes, as in "During our term, we distributed three million acres."

Fourth. Never use one diminutive if you can use five in a row.

Fifth. Never use the imperative when you can use the subjunctive.

Sixth. And only then, when you have exhausted these ceremonies of communication, bring out your verbal knife and plunge
it deep into the other's heart: "Chinga a tu madre, cabrón."

The language of Mexicans is born from abysmal extremes of
power and impotence, domination and resentment: it is the mirror
of an overabundance of history, a history that devours itself before
burning itself and then re-generating itself, phoenix-like, once
more.

Argentina, on the contrary, is a *tabula rasa* and it demands
a passionate verbalization. I do not know another country that so
fervently — with the fervor of Buenos Aires, Borges would say —
opposes the silence of its infinite space, its physical and mental
pampa, demanding: please, *verbalize* me!

Martin Fierro, Carlos Gardel, Jorge Luis Borges: reality must
be captured, desperately, in the verbal web of the gaucho poem,
the sentimental tango or the metaphysical tale: the pampa of the
gaucho becomes the garden of the tango becomes the forked paths
of literature.

What is forked? What is said.

What is said? What is forked.

Everything: Space. Time. Language. History. Our history.
The history of Spanish America.

I read *Ficciones* as I flew north on a pontoon plane courtesy of
Pan American Airways. It was wartime, we had to have priority;
all cameras were banned and glazed plastic screens were put on
our windows several minutes before we landed. Since I was not
an Axis spy I read Borges as we splashed into Santos, saying that
the best proof that the Koran is an Arab book is that not a single
camel is mentioned in its pages. I started thinking that the best
proof that Borges is an Argentinian is in everything that he has
to evoke because it isn't there, as we glided into an invisible
Rio de Janeiro. And as we flew out of Bahía, I thought that
Borges invents a world because he needs it. I need, therefore I
imagine.

By the time we landed in Trinidad, the reading of "Funes the Memorious" and "Pierre Ménard, Author of Don Quixote" had introduced me, without my knowledge, to the genealogy of the serene madmen, the children of Erasmus. I did not know then that this was the most illustrious family of modern fiction, since it went, backwards, from Pierre Ménard to Don Quixote himself. During two short lulls in Santo Domingo (then, horrifyingly, called Ciudad Trujillo) and Port-au-Prince, I had been prepared in Borges to encounter my wonderful friends Toby Shandy, who reconstructs in his miniature cabbage patch the battlefields of Flanders he can no longer live in history; Jane Austen's Catherine Moreland and Gustave Flaubert's Madame Bovary, who like Don Quixote believe in what they read; Dickens' Mr. Micawber, who takes his hopes to be realities; Dostoevsky's Myshkin, an idiot because he gives the benefit of the doubt to the good possibility of mankind; Perez Galdos' Nazarín, who is mad because he believes that each human being can be a daily Christ and is truly Saint Paul's madman:

> Let him who seems wise among you become mad,
> so that he might truly become wise.

On landing at Miami Airport the glazed windows disappeared once and for all and I knew that like Pierre Ménard a writer must always face the mysterious duty of literally reconstructing a spontaneous work. And so I met my tradition: *Don Quixote* was a book waiting to be written. The history of Latin America was a history waiting to be lived.

III

When I finally arrived in Mexico, I discovered that my father's imaginary country was real, but more fantastic than any imaginary land. It was as real as its physical and spiritual borders: Mexico, the only frontier between the industrialized and the developing worlds; the frontier between my country and the United States but also between all of Latin America and the United States, as between the Mediterranean and the Anglo-Saxon strains in the New World, between the thrift of Protestantism and the prodigality of Catholicism, between the horizontal and extensive decentralization of power and its absolutist, pyramidal, and centralized structure, between customary, unwritten law and the Roman law tradition, where nothing exists unless it is written down.

You are the children of the heretic Pelagius, who believed in direct grace between God and Man; we, of the orthodox Saint Augustine who believed that grace is achieved only through the mediation of hierarchy. You are founded on the parsimony of capitalism. We are founded on an autocratic and populist dispensation. You peer at your ledgers through the spectacles of Ben Franklin. We spend our wealth on altars and rockets, like Philip II. Your art has the nameless simplicity of a New England church; ours has the baroque abundance of gold leaf in a flea-bitten village. You represent the poverty of wealth; we the wealth of poverty.

You want to live better. We want to die better. You feel that you must redeem the future. We are convinced that we must redeem the past. Your past is assimilated; at times, one would fear, it is even forgotten. Ours is still battling for our souls. You are accustomed to success; we, to failure. Or, rather, your failures drive you to a self-flagellating malaise of incomprehension. Mexico measures its successes with the tragic misgivings of experience; all things in life are limited and fleeting, especially success.

Some day North Americans shall ask themselves how to transform Pocahontas into the Virgin of Guadalupe, and Mexicans shall ask themselves, can you transform Moctezuma into a member of the Kennedy dynasty? How can you make a ritual out of eating a hamburger? Can you sell *mole poblano* by computer?

How to say, in Spanish, "To be or not to be?," when in English we cannot distinguish our *ser* from our *estar*?

It was with this experience and these questions that I approached the body of gold and mud of Mexico, the imaginary, imagined country, finally real but only real if I saw it from a distance which would assure me, thanks to the fact of separation, that my desire for reunion with it would be forever urgent and only real if I wrote it. Thanks to perspective I was, finally, able to write a few novels where I could speak of the scars of revolution, the nightmares of progress, and the perseverance of dreams.

I wrote urgently because my absence became a destiny, yet a shared destiny: that of my own body as a young man, that of the old body of my country and that of the problematic and insomniac body of my language.

I could, perhaps, identify the former without too much trouble: Mexico and myself. But the language belonged to us all, to the vast community that writes and talks and thinks in Spanish. And without this language I could give no reality to either myself or my land. Language thus became the center of my personal being and of my possibility of transforming my own destiny and that of my country into a shared destiny.

But nothing is shared in the abstract. Like bread and love, language and ideas are shared with human beings.

My first contact with literature was sitting on the knees of Alfonso Reyes when the Mexican writer was Ambassador to Brazil in the earlier thirties. Reyes had brought the Spanish classics back to life for us; he had written the most superb books on Greece; he was the most lucid of literary theoreticians; in fact, he had translated all of Western culture into Latin American terms. In the late forties, he was living in a little house the color of the *mamey* fruit in Cuernavaca. He would invite me to spend weekends with him and since I was eighteen and a night-prowler I only accompanied him from eleven in the morning, when don Alfonso would sit in a cafe and throw verbal flowers at the girls strolling around the plaza that was then a garden of laurels and not, as it has become, of cement; I do not know if the square, ruddy man seated at the next table was a British consul crushed by the vicinity of the volcano; but if Reyes, enjoying the spectacle of the world, would quote Lope de Vega and Garcilaso, our neighbour the *mescal* drinker would answer, without looking at us, with the more somber *stanze* of Marlowe and John Donne. Then we would go to the movies in order, Reyes said, to take a bath in contemporary epic, and only at night would he start scolding me, how come you have not read Stendhal yet?, the world didn't start five minutes ago, you know.

He could irritate me; I read, against his classical tastes, the most modern, the most strident books, without understanding that I was learning his lesson: there is no creation without tradition, the "new" is an inflection on a preceding form, novelty is always a work on the past.

Borges said of him that Reyes wrote the best Spanish prose of our times. He taught me that culture had a smile; that the intellectual tradition of the whole world was ours by birthright and that Mexican literature was important because it was literature, not because it was Mexican.

One day I got up very early (or maybe I came in very late from a binge) and saw him seated at five in the morning, working at his table, surrounded by the renewed aromas of the jacaranda and the bougainvillea. He was a diminutive Buddha, bald and pink, almost one of those elves who cobble shoes at night while the family sleeps. He liked to quote Goethe: Write at dawn, skim the cream of the day, then you can study crystals, intrigue at court, and make love to your kitchen-maid. Writing in silence, Reyes did not smile: his world, in a way, ended on a funeral day in February 1913, when his insurrected father, General Bernardo Reyes, fell riddled by machine gun bullets in the Zocalo in Mexico City and with him fell whatever was left of Mexico's Belle Epoque, the long and cruel peace of Porfirio Díaz.

The smile of Alfonso Reyes had ashes in its lips. He had written, as a response to history, the great poem of exile and dis-

tance from Mexico: the poem of a cruel Iphigenia, the Mexican
Iphigenia of the valley of Anáhuac:

> I was another, being myself;
> I was he who wanted to leave.
> To return is to cry. I do not repent of this wide world.
> It is not I who return,
> But my shackled feet.

My father had remained in Buenos Aires as Mexican *chargé
d'affaires*, with instructions to frown at Argentina's sympathies
towards the Axis. My mother profited from his absence by enroll-
ing me in a Catholic school in Mexico City. The brothers who
ruled this institution were extremely preoccupied with something
that had never entered my head: s-i-n, *Sin*. On the inauguration
of the school year, one of the brothers would appear before the
class with a white lily in his hand and say: "This is a Catholic
youth before kissing a girl." Then he would throw the flower on
the floor, dance a little jig on it, pick up the bedraggled vegetable,
and confirm our worst suspicions: "This is a Catholic boy after . . ."

Well, all of this made life very tempting and, retrospectively,
I would agree with Luis Buñuel when he says that sex without sin
is like an egg without salt. The priests at the Colegio Francés
made sex irresistible for us; they also made leftists of us by their
constant denunciation of Mexican liberalism and, especially, of
Benito Juárez. The sexual and political temptations became very
great in a city where provincial mores and sharp social distinction
made it extremely difficult to have normal sexual relationships
with young or even older women.

All this led, as I say, to a posture of rebellion that for me
crystallized in the decision to be a writer. My father, by then back
from Argentina, sternly said, OK, then go out and be a writer,
but not at my expense. I became a very young journalist in the
weekly *Siempre*, but my family pressured me to enter law school,
or, in the desert of Mexican literature, I would literally die of

hunger and thirst. Again, I was sent to visit Alfonso Reyes in his enormous library-house, where he seemed more diminutive than ever, ensconced in a tiny corner he saved for his bed among the Piranesi-like perspective of the volumes piled upon volumes, and he said to me: "Mexico is a very formalistic country. If you don't have a title, you are nobody: *nadie, ninguno.* A title is like the handle on a cup; without it, no one will pick you up. You must become a *licenciado,* a lawyer; then you can do whatever you please, like I did."

So I entered the School of Law at the National University, where, as I feared, learning tended to be by rote. The budding explosion in the student population was compounded by cynical teachers who would spend the whole hour of class passing list on the two hundred students of Civil Law, from Aguilar to Zapata. But there were great exceptions of true teachers who understood that the Law was inseparable from a culture, from morality, and from justice. Foremost among these were the exiles from the defeat of Republican Spain who had enormously enriched Mexican universities, publishing houses, the arts, and the sciences. Don Manuel Pedroso, former dean of the University of Seville, made the study of Law compatible with my literary inclinations. When I would bitterly complain about the dryness and boredom of learning the penal or mercantile codes by heart, he would counter by saying: "Forget the codes. Read Dostoevsky, read Balzac. There's all you have to know about criminal or commercial law." He also made me understand that Stendhal was right when he said that the best model for a well-structured novel is the Napoleonic Code of Civil Law. Anyway, I found that culture is made of connections, not of separations: to specialize is to isolate.

Sex was another story, but Mexico City was then a manageable town of one million people, beautiful in its extremes of colonial and nineteenth-century elegance and the garishness of its exuberant and dangerous nightlife. My friends and I spent away the last years of our adolescence and the first of our manhood in a succession of cantinas, brothels, strip-joints and silver-painted nightclubs where the bolero was sung and the mambo danced; whores, mariachis, magicians, were our constant companions as we struggled through our first readings of D. H. Lawrence and Aldous Huxley, James Joyce and André Gide, T. S. Eliot and Thomas Mann. Salvador Elizondo and I were the two would-be writers of the group, and if the realistic grain of *La región más transparente* was sown in this our rather somnambulistic immersion in the spectral nightlife of Mexico City, it is also true that the cruel imagination of an instant in Elizondo's *Farabeuf* had the same background experience. We would go to a whorehouse strangely called El Buen Tono, choose a poor Mexican girl who usually said her name was Gladys and she came from Guadalajara and go to our respective rooms. A horrible scream would then be heard and Gladys from Guadalajara would rush out, crying and streaming blood. Elizondo, in the culmination of love, had slashed her armpit with a razor.

Another perspective, another distance for approximation, another possibility of sharing a language. In 1950 I went to Europe to do graduate work in international law at the University in Geneva. Octavio Paz had just published two books that had changed the face of Mexican literature, *Libertad bajo palabra* and *El laberinto de la soledad*. My friends and I had read those books out loud in Mexico, dazzled by a poetics that managed, simultaneously, to renew our language from within and then connect it to the language of the world.

At age thirty-six, Octavio Paz was not very different from what he is today. Writers born in 1914, like Paz and Julio Cortázar, surely signed a Faustian pact at the very mouth of hell's trenches; so many poets died in that war that someone had to take their place. I remember Paz in the so-called existentialist nightclubs of the time in Paris, in discussion with the very animated and handsome Albert Camus, who alternated philosophy and the boogie-woogie in La Rose Rouge; I remember Paz in front of the

large windows of a gallery on the Place Vendôme, reflecting Max
Ernst's great postwar painting, "Europe after the rain" and the
painter's profile as an ancient eagle, and I tell myself that the
poetics of Paz is an art of civilizations, a movement of encoun-
ters: Paz the poet meets Paz the thinker, because his poetry is a
form of thought and his thought is a form of poetry; and thanks
to this meeting, the encounter of different civilizations takes place:
Paz introduces civilizations to one another, makes them present-
able before it is too late, because behind the wonderful smile of
Camus, fixed forever in the absurdity of death, behind the bright
erosion of painting by Max Ernst and the crystals of the Place
Vendôme, Octavio and I, when we met, could hear the voice of
el poeta Libra, Ezra, lamenting the death of the best, "for an old
bitch gone in the teeth, for a botched civilization."

Octavio Paz has offered civilizations the mirror of their mor-
tality, as Paul Valéry did, but also the reflection of their arrival
in an epidemic of meetings and erotic risks. In the generous
friendship of Octavio Paz I learnt that there were no privileged
centers of culture, race, or politics; that nothing should be left out
of literature because our time is a time of deadly reduction. The
essential orphanhood of our time is seen by the poetry and thought
of Paz as a challenge to be met through the renewed flux of human
knowledge, of *all* human knowledge. We have not finished thinking, imagining, acting. It is still possible to know the world; we
are unfinished men and women.

> I am not at the crossroads;
> to choose is to err
>
> . . .
>
> I am in a cage hanging from time . . .

For my generation in Mexico the problem did not consist in
discovering our modernity, but in discovering our tradition. The
latter was brutally denied by the comatose, petrified teaching of
the classics in Mexican high schools: one had to bring Cervantes

back to life in spite of a school system fatally oriented towards the idea of universities as sausage factories. It was also denied by the more grotesque forms of Mexican nationalism at the time. A Marxist teacher once told me it was un-Mexican to read Kafka; a fascist critic said the same thing (this has been Kafka's Kafkian destiny everywhere, you know), and a rather sterile Mexican author gave a pompous lecture at the Bellas Artes warning that readers who read Proust would proustitute themselves.

To be a writer in Mexico in the fifties you had to be with Reyes and with Paz in the assertion that Mexico was not an isolated, virginal province, but very much a part of the human race and its cultural tradition; that we were all, for good or for evil, contemporary to all men and women.

In Geneva I regained my perspective. I rented a garret overlooking the beautiful old square of the Bourg-du-Four, founded by Julius Caesar as the Forum Boarium two millennia ago. The square was filled with coffeehouses and old bookstores. The girls came from all over the world, they were beautiful and they were independent. When they were kissed, one did not become a sullied lily. We had salt on our lips. We loved one another and I also loved going to the little island where the lake meets the river to spend long hours reading. Since it was called the Jean Jacques Rousseau Island, I took along my volume of the *Confessions*. Many things came together then. A novel was the transformation of experience into history. The modern epic had been the epic of the first-person singular, of the I, from St. Augustine to Abelard to Dante to Rousseau to Stendhal to Proust. Joyce de-voiced fiction: Here Comes Everybody! But H. C. E. did not collectively save the degraded Ego from exhaustion, self-doubt and, finally, self-forgetfullness. When Odysseus sees he is inexistent, we know and he knows that he is disguised; when Beckett's characters proclaim their non-being, we know that "the fact is notorious": they are no longer disguised. Kafka's man has been forgotten; no one can remember K the land surveyor; finally, as Milan

Kundera tells us, nobody can remember Prague, Czechoslovakia, History.

I did not yet know this as I spent many reading hours on the little island of Rousseau on the intersection of Lake Geneva and the Rhône River back in 1951. But I obscurely felt that there was something beyond the exploration of the self that actually made the idea of human personality possible if the paths beyond it were explored. Cervantes taught us that book is a book is a book: Don Quixote does not invite us into "reality," but into an act of the imagination where all things are real: the characters are active psychological entities, but also the archetypes they announce and always the figures from whence they came and that were un-imaginable, un-thinkable, as Don Quixote, before they became characters first and archetypes later.

Could I, a Mexican who had not yet written his first book, sitting on a bench on an early spring's day, as the *bisse* from the Jura Mountains quieted down, have the courage to explore for myself, with my language, with my tradition, with my friends and influences, that region where the figure bids us consider it in the insecurity of its gestation? Cervantes did it in a precise cultural situation: he inaugurated the modern world by making Don Quixote leave the village of his security (but a village whose name has been, let us remember, forgotten) and take to the roads of the unsheltered, the unknown and the different, there to lose what he read, and to gain what we, the readers, read in him.

The novel is forever travelling Don Quixote's road, from the security of the analogous to the adventure of the different and, even, the unknown. In my way, this is the road I wanted to travel. I read Rousseau, or the adventures of the I; Joyce and Faulkner, or the adventures of the We; Cervantes, or the adventures of the You he calls the Idle, the Amiable Reader: you. And I read, in a shower of fire and in the lightning of enthusiasm, Rimbaud. His mother asked him what this poem was about. And he answered: "I have wanted to say what it says there, literally and in all other senses."

This statement by Rimbaud has always been a demanding rule for me and for what we are all writing today; and the present-day vigor in the literature of the Hispanic world, to which I belong, is not alien to this Rimbaldian approach to writing: Say what you mean, literally and in all other senses.

I think I imagined in Switzerland what I would try to write some day but would first have to pay my apprenticeship and only be able to write what I then imagined after many years, when I not only knew that I had the tools with which to do it, but also, and equally important, when I knew that if I did not write, death would not write it for me. You start by writing to live. You end by writing not to die. Love is the actual marriage of this desire and of this fear. The women I have loved I have desired for themselves, but also because I feared myself.

IV

My first European experience came to a climax in the summer of 1950. It was a hot and calm evening on Lake Zurich and some wealthy Mexican friends had invited me to dinner at the elegant Bar-au-Lac Hotel. The summer restaurant was a floating terrace on the lake. You reached it by a gangplank and it was lighted by paper lanterns and flickering candles. As I unfolded my stiff white napkin among the soothing tinkle of silver and glass, I raised my eyes and saw the group dining at the next table.

Three ladies sat there with a man in his seventies. This man was stiff and elegant, dressed in double-breasted white serge and immaculate shirt and tie. His long, delicate fingers sliced a cold pheasant, almost, with daintiness. Yet even in eating he seemed to me seemingly unbending, with a ramrod-backed, military sort of bearing. The age of his face showed "a growing fatigue," but the pride with which his lips and his jaws were set tried desperately to hide the fact, while the eyes twinkled with "the fiery play of fancy."

As the carnival lights of that summer's night in Zurich played with a fire of their own on the features I now recognized, Thomas Mann's face was a theater of implicit, quiet emotions. He ate and let the ladies do the talking; he was, in my fascinated eyes, a meeting place where solitude gives birth to beauty unfamiliar and perilous, but also to the perverse and the illicit. Thomas Mann had managed, out of this solitude, to find the affinity "between the personal destiny of [the] author and that of his contemporaries in general." Through him, I had imagined that the products of this solitude and of this affinity were named art (created by one) and civilization (created by all). He spoke so surely, in *Death in Venice*, of the "tasks imposed upon him by his own ego and the European soul," that as I saw him there that night, paralyzed with admiration, I dared not conceive of such an affinity in our own Latin American culture, where the extreme demands of a ravaged, voiceless continent often killed the voice of the self and rendered a hollow political monster, or killed the voice of the society and gave birth to a pitiful, sentimental dwarf.

Yet, as I recalled my passionate readings of everything he wrote, from *Blood of the Walsungs* to *Doktor Faustus*, I could not help but feel that, in spite of the vast differences between his culture and ours, in both of them literature always asserted itself through a relationship between the visible and invisible worlds of the narration. A novel should "gather up the threads of many human destinies in the warp of a single idea"; the I, the You, and the We were only separated and dried up because of a lack of imagination.

I left Thomas Mann, unbeknownst to him, sipping his demitasse as midnight approached and the floating restaurant bobbed slightly and the Chinese lanterns quietly flickered out. I shall always thank him for silently teaching me that, in literature, you only know what you imagine.

The Mexico of the forties and fifties I wrote about in *La región más transparente* was an imagined Mexico, just as the Mexico of the eighties and nineties I am writing about in "Cristóbal Nonato" is totally imagined. I fear that we would know nothing of Balzac's Paris and Dickens' London if they too had not invented them. When in the spring of 1951 I took a Dutch steamer back to the New World, I carried with me the ten Bible-paper tomes of the Pléiade edition of Balzac. This phrase of his has been a central belief of mine: "Wrest words from silence and ideas from obscurity." The reading of Balzac — one of the most thorough and metamorphosing experiences of my life as a novelist — taught me that one must exhaust reality, transcend it in order to reach — to try to reach — that absolute which is made of the atoms of the relative: in Balzac, the marvelous worlds of *Séraphita* or *Louis Lambert* rest on the commonplace worlds of *Père Goriot* and *César Birotteau*. Likewise, the Mexican reality of *La región más transparente* and *La muerte de Artemio Cruz* existed only to clash with my imagination, my negation, and my perversion of the facts because, remember, I had learnt to *imagine* Mexico before I ever *knew* Mexico.

This was, finally, a way of ceasing to tell what I understood and trying to tell, behind all the things I knew, the really important things: what I did not know. *Aura* illustrates this stance much too clearly, I suppose. I prefer to find it in a scene set in a cantina in *A Change of Skin*, or in a taxi drive in *The Hydra Head*. I never wanted to resolve an enigma, but to point out that there *was* an enigma.

I always tried to ask my critics, "Don't classify me, read me. I'm a writer, not a genre. Do not look for the purity of the novel according to some nostalgic canon, do not ask for generic affiliation but rather for a dialogue, if not for the outright abolition of genre; not for one language but for many languages at odds with one another; not, as Bakhtin would put it, for unity of style but for *heteroglossia*, not for monologic but for dialogic imagination."

I'm afraid that, by and large, in Mexico, at least, I failed in this enterprise. Yet I am not disturbed by this fact, because of what I have just said: language is a shared and sharing part of culture that cares little about formal classifications and much about vitality and connection, for culture itself perishes in purity or isolation, which is the deadly wages of perfection. Like bread and love, language is shared with others. And human beings share a tradition. There is no creation without tradition. No one creates from nothing.

I went back to Mexico but knew that I would forever be a wanderer in search of perspective: this was my real baptism, not the religious or the civil ceremonies I have mentioned. But no matter where I went, Spanish would be the language of my writing and Latin America the culture of my language.

Neruda, Reyes, Paz; Washington, Santiago de Chile, Buenos Aires, Mexico City, Paris, Geneva; Cervantes, Balzac, Rimbaud, Thomas Mann: only with all the shared languages, those of my places and friends and masters, was I able to approach the body of fire of literature and ask it for a few sparks.

We are not alone. To write in Spanish and in Spanish America is no longer an act of isolated eccentricity. It belongs to, it leans on, a tradition. We all write, as Virginia Woolf demands of the European writer, with a feeling that all the writers since Homer are there, present in our bones as we write. When Alfonso Reyes was asked what the influences on the then-young Mexican writers Juan Rulfo and Juan José Arreola had been, he answered, "Two thousand years of literature."

Homer: we could add the Popol Vuh; Quetzalcoatl and Ulysses; Athens and the African Kalahari the Puerto Rican poet Luis Palés Matos sings about:

> Where did this word come from,
> Hidden like an insect in my memory?
> and now alive, insistent,
> fluttering blindly
> against the blinding light of memory?

From its very foundation, Latin America has a profound continuity of culture and a constant fragmentation of history. An uninterrupted culture and a sporadic society; unity of civilization and political Balkanization; a triumph of art and a failure of history.

We require a model of progress of our own, not an extralogical imitation as in the more fragile errors of our history, but a critical model of our own, pertaining to our own culture, Indian, European, Black, Mestizo. This vast project of regeneration of a prostrate and vitiated continent includes the rights and obligations of literature.

The paradox of writing in a continent ravaged by illiteracy is perhaps not so great; perhaps the writer knows that he writes in order to keep alive that prodigious cultural past that rarely found historical equivalency. To write in a continent of illiterates. Indeed. And if to write now were but to communicate with those who, one day, will no longer be illiterate and will then have the right to reclaim the absent voices of today as we reclaim those of the past, to demand the *Hopscotch* that should have been published in 1963, the *Labyrinth of Solitude* that should have been published in 1950, the *Residence on Earth* that should have been published in 1933, the *Hundred Years of Solitude* that should have been published in 1967, but were not, because, then, only an elite would have read them, and, after all, the elite preferred to read bad translations of European novels. Whoever heard of Cortázar or Paz, or Neruda or García Márquez? Maybe they were silent and obscure, unpublished humorists who lived out the eighteenth century in a gaucho trading post in Tucumán, in a pink cobbled square in Mixcoac, on a foggy, rainy farm near Temuco, or on a slow boat chugging up the Magdalena River towards another heart of darkness? We don't know; we were reading *Clarissa Harlowe*.

And if to write today, always, in Spanish America were to offer but another level, another relief, to that constant territory of our civilization: the uninterrupted presence of a strong popular

culture, manual, artisinal, a singing, dancing, coloring, construc-
ing culture? Who built Chichén Itzá and Machu Picchu, Torre
Tagle in Lima and La Compañía in Quito? Our life depends on
knowing this: either we say they are ghosts because we ignore our
past and become ghosts ourselves, or we say they were human
beings because we know our past and become human beings
ourselves.

To say, with the poem, the novel, the essay, all that which
has not been said by a deformed history and a mutilated polity.

And to say it in the language which is common to us all: the
Spanish language.

We shall never let it go dead on us again: this is the great
challenge of our generation of writers.

We shall never permit the great language of Cervantes to play
the play of the Sleeping Beauty again.

We shall wake her up with our fists, we will kick her, we will
slap her around.

We will hopscotch the language.

We will onehundredyearsofsolitudinize it.

We will reside it on earth, paradise it, explode it in a cathedral,
alephize it, betray it with Rita Hayworth, feed it to the obscure
bird of night and let the three trapped tigers devour it.

Catch them by the tail, says Octavio Paz, capture them, rip
them open, make the sluts scream: the words, our words, once
more.

Let us not lose them again, because now we have our words
counted.

Only an Illusion

ILYA PRIGOGINE

THE TANNER LECTURES ON HUMAN VALUES

Delivered at
Jawaharlal Nehru University

December 18, 1982

ILYA PRIGOGINE was born in Moscow and is now a citizen of Belgium. He received his doctorate in science from the Université Libre de Bruxelles in 1941 and has been Professor at that institution since 1951. Since 1959 he has been Director of the Instituts Internationaux de Physique et de Chimie, fondés par E. Solvay, and, since 1967, Regents' Professor of Physics and Chemical Engineering at the Center for Statistical Mechanics and Thermodynamics of the University of Texas at Austin. In 1981 he was appointed Special Advisor to the Commission of the European Communities.

Professor Prigogine's most recent work in English is *From Being to Becoming: Time and Complexity in the Physical Sciences*; his monographs have been translated into many languages. He has received eleven honorary degrees and numerous scientific awards and medals; in 1977, Professor Prigogine was awarded the Nobel Prize in Chemistry.

1

Let me start with a recollection of Werner Heisenberg when, as a young man, he took a walking tour with Niels Bohr. This is Heisenberg's account of what Bohr said when they came to Kronberg Castle.

Isn't it strange how this castle changes as soon as one imagines that Hamlet lived here? As scientists we believe that a castle consists only of stones, and admire the way the architect put them together. The stones, the green roof with its patina, the wood carvings in the church, constitute the whole castle. None of this should be changed by the fact that Hamlet lived here, and yet it is changed completely. Suddenly the walls and the ramparts speak a different language . . . . Yet all we really know about Hamlet is that his name appears in a thirteenth-century chronicle . . . . But everyone knows the questions Shakespeare had him ask, the human depths he was made to reveal, and so he too had to be found a place on earth, here in Kronberg.[1]

Obviously this story brings us to a question which is as old as humanity itself: *the meaning of reality.*

This question cannot be dissociated from another one, the meaning of time. To us time and human existence, and therefore also reality, are concepts which are undissociable. But is this necessarily so? I like to quote the correspondence between Einstein and his old friend Besso. In the latter years Besso comes back again and again to the question of time. What is time, what is irreversibility? Patiently Einstein answers again and again, irreversibility is an *illusion,* a subjective impression, coming from exceptional initial conditions.

[1] Gordon Mills, *Hamlet's Castle* (Austin: University of Texas Press, 1976).

[37]

Besso's death only a few months before Einstein's own was to interrupt this correspondence. At Besso's death, in a moving letter to Besso's sister and son, Einstein wrote: "Michele has preceded me a little in leaving this strange world. This is not important. For us who are convinced physicists, the distinction between past, present, and future is only an illusion, however persistent." [2]

"Only an illusion." I must confess that this sentence has greatly impressed me. It seems to me that it expresses in an exceptionally striking way the symbolic power of the mind.

In fact, in his letter Einstein was reiterating what Giordano Bruno had written in the sixteenth century and what had become for centuries the credo of science.

> *The universe is, therefore, one, infinite, immobile.* One, I say, is the absolute possibility, one the act, one the form or soul, one the matter or body, one the thing, one the being, one the maximum and optimum; which is not capable of being comprehended; and yet is without end and interminable, and to that extent infinite and interminate, and consequently immobile. *It does not move itself locally*, because it has nothing outside itself to which it might be transported, it being understood that it is all. *It does not generate itself* since there is no other thing into which it could desire or look for, it being understood that it has all the beings. *It is not corruptible*, since there is no other thing into which it could change itself, it being understood that it is everything. It cannot diminish or increase, it being understood that it is infinite, thus being that to which nothing can be added, and that from which nothing can be subtracted, for the reason that the universe does not have proportional parts. *It is not alterable* into any other disposition because it does not have anything external through which it could suffer and through which it could be affected. [3]

---

[2] Einstein–Besso, *Correspondance*, ed. by Speziali (Paris: Herman, 1972), pp. 537–39.

[3] G. Bruno, 5ème dialogue, *De la causa, Opere Italiane*, I (Bari 1907); cf. I. Leclerc, *The Nature of Physical Existence* (London: George Allen & Unwin, 1972), p. 88.

For a long time Bruno's vision was to dominate the scientific view of the western world. It was to lead to the "mechanical world view with its two basic elements":

a. changeless substances such as atoms, molecules or elementary particles;

b. locomotion.[4]

Of course many changes came through quantum theory, to which I shall return, but some basic features of this conception remain even now. But how to understand this timeless nature which puts man outside the reality he describes? As Carl Rubino has emphasized, Homer's *Iliad* centers around the problem of time. Achilles *embarks in a search for something permanent and immutable*. "But the wisdom of the *Iliad*, a bitter lesson that Achilles, its hero, learns too late, is that such perfection can be gained only at the cost of one's humanity: he must lose his life in order to gain this new degree of glory. For human men and women, *for us*, immutability, freedom from change, total security, immunity from life's maddening ups and downs will come only when we depart this life, by dying, or becoming gods: the gods, Horace tells us, are the only living beings who lead secure lives, free from anxiety and change." [5]

Homer's *Odyssey* appears as the dialectical counterpart to the *Iliad*.[6] Odysseus has the choice; he is fortunate enough to be able to choose between agelessness, immortality — remaining forever the lover of Calypso — or the return to humanity, and ultimately to old age and death: Still he chooses time over eternity, human's fate over god's fate.

Let us still stay in literature but come closer to our time. In his *Cimetière marin* Paul Valéry describes man's struggle to come

[4] Ibid.

[5] Carl Rubino, "Winged chariots and black holes: Some reflexions on science and literature," preprint.

[6] J. P. Vernant, "Le refus d'Ulysse," *Le temps de la réflexion* III (1982).

to terms with time as duration, with its limited span open to us.
In his "Cahiers" — those numerous volumes of notes he used to
write in the early mornings — he comes back again and again to
the problem of time: Duration, science to be constructed.[7] There is a
deep feeling for the unexpected in Valéry, why things are happening as they do. Obviously Valéry could not be satisfied with
simple explanations such as schemes implying a universal determinism which supposes that in some sense *all is given.* Valéry
writes:

> Le déterminisme — subtil anthropomorphisme — dit que tout
> se passe comme dans une machine telle qu'elle est comprise
> par moi. Mais toute loi mécanique est au fond irrationnelle —
> expérimentale. . . . Le *sens du mot déterminisme est du même
> degré de vague que celui du mot liberté. . . . Le déterminisme
> rigoureux est profondément déiste. Car il faudrait un dieu
> pour apercevoir cet enchaînement infini complet.* Il faut
> imaginer un dieu, un front de dieu pour imaginer cette
> logique. C'est un point de vue divin. De sorte que le dieu
> retranché de la création et de l'invention de l'univers est
> restitué pour la compréhension de cet univers. Qu'on le veuille
> ou non, un dieu est posé nécessairement dans la pensée du
> déterminisme — et c'est une rigoureuse ironie.[8]

Valéry is making an important remark to which I shall return — determinism is only possible for an observer outside his
world, while we describe the world from within.

---

[7] Paul Valéry, *Cahiers* I (1973), II (1974), Bibliothèque de la Pléiade (Paris:
Editions Gallimard).

[8] Paul Valéry, *Cahiers* I, pp. 492, 531, 651: "Determinism — subtle anthropo-
morphism — says that everything occurs as if in a machine as understood by myself.
But every mechanical law is irrational at base — experimental. . . . *The meaning of
the word determinism is vague to the same degree as that of the word freedom. . . .
Rigid determinism is profoundly deistic.* Because you have to have a god to be able
to see the entire infinite chain. It is necessary to imagine a god, the face of a god, to
be able to imagine this logic. It is a divine point of view. So that the god who was
confined to the creation of the universe is reinstated in order to understand this universe. Whether one likes it or not, a god is a requisite part of the idea of determinism — and this is a harsh irony."

This preoccupation with time in Valéry is not an isolated phenomenon in the early part of this century. We may quote in disorder Proust, Bergson, Teilhard, Freud, Peirce or Whitehead. As we have mentioned, the verdict of science seemed final. Time *is* an illusion. Still again and again the question was asked: how is this possible? Do we have really to make a tragic choice between a timeless reality which leads to human alienation or an affirmation of time which seems to brade with scientific rationality?

Most of European philosophy from Kant to Whitehead appears as an attempt to overcome in one way or another the necessity of this choice.[9] We cannot go into detail, but obviously Kant's distinction between a noumenal world and a phenomenal one was a step in this direction, as is Whitehead's idea of process philosophy. None of these attempts has met with more than a mitigated success. As a result, we have seen a progressive decay of "philosophy of nature." I agree completely with Leclerc when he writes: "In the present century we are suffering the consequences of the separation of science and philosophy which followed upon the triumph of Newtonian physics in the eighteenth century. It is not only the dialogue between science and philosophy which has suffered."[10]

Here is one of the roots of the dichotomy into "two cultures." There is an irreducible opposition between classical *reason* with its nontemporal vision and our *existence* with its vision of time as this *twirl* which Nabokov describes in *Look at the Harlequins*.[11] But something very dramatic is happening in science — something as unexpected as the birth of geometry, or the grandiose vision of the cosmos as expressed in Newton's work. We become progressively more and more conscious of the fact that, on all levels

[9] I. Prigogine and I. Stengers, *La Nouvelle Alliance* (Paris: Gallimard, 1979); German trans. Piper, Italian trans. Einaudi, English translation to appear in 1983.

[10] *The Nature of Physical Existence*, p. 31.

[11] New York: McGraw-Hill, 1981; cf. M. Gardner, *The Ambidextrous Universe* (New York: Charles Scribner's Sons, 1979).

from elementary particles up to cosmology, science is rediscovering time.

We are still embedded in this process of reconceptualization of physics — we still don't know where it will lead. But certainly it opens a new chapter in the dialogue between men and nature. In this perspective the problem of the relation between science and human values, the central subject of the Tanner Lectures, can be seen in a new perspective. A dialogue between natural sciences, human sciences, including arts and literature, may take a new start and perhaps develop into something as fruitful as it was during the classical period of Greece or during the seventeenth century, at the time of Newton and Leibniz.

II

To understand the changes which are going on in our time, it may be useful to start with our scientific heritage from the nineteenth century. I believe that this heritage included *two basic contradictions* or at least *two basic questions* to which no answer was provided.

As you know, the nineteenth century was essentially the century of evolution. Think about the work of Darwin in biology, of Hegel in philosophy, or of the formulation of the famous entropy law in physics.

Let us start with *Darwin*. The present year is the centenary of the death of Darwin. Beyond the importance of *The Origin of Species*, published in 1859, for biological evolution proper, there is a general element involved in Darwin's approach which I want to emphasize.[12] His approach combines *two* elements: the assumption of spontaneous *fluctuations* in biological species, which then through selection from the medium lead to *irreversible* biological evolution. Therefore, his model combines two elements to which

[12] M. Peckham, *Charles Darwin; The Origin of Species, in the Variorum Text* (Philadelphia: University of Pennsylvania Press, 1959).

we shall very often return in this lecture: the idea of *fluctuations*, or randomness, of stochastic processes, and the idea of evolution, of *irreversibility*. Let us emphasize that on the level of biology this association leads to evolution corresponding to increasing complexity, to self-organization.

This is in complete contrast to the meaning which is generally associated with the law of *entropy* increase as formulated by Clausius in 1865.[13] The basic element in this law is the distinction between reversible and irreversible processes. Reversible processes do not know any privileged direction of time. You may think about a spring oscillating in a frictionless medium or about planetary motion. On the other hand, irreversible processes involve an arrow of time. If you bring together two liquids they tend to mix, but the unmixing is not observed as a spontaneous process. All of chemistry corresponds to irreversible processes. This distinction is taken up in the formulation of the second law, which postulates the existence of a function, entropy, which in an isolated system can only increase because of the presence of irreversible processes while itself remaining unchanged through reversible processes. Therefore, in an isolated system, entropy will finally reach its maximum whenever the system has come to equilibrium and the irreversible processes to a final halt.

It is the work of one of the greatest theoretical physicists of all time, Ludwig Boltzmann, that gave a first microscopic interpretation to this increase of entropy. He turned to kinetic theory of gases with the idea that the mechanism of change, of "evolution" is then described in terms of collisions between molecules. His main conclusion was that entropy S closely related to *probability* P. Everybody has heard quoted the famous formula $S = k \, ln \, P$, which was engraved on Boltzmann's tombstone after his tragic suicide in 1906.[14] Here k is a universal constant named

---

[13] See Prigogine and Stengers, *La Nouvelle Alliance*.

[14] I. Prigogine, *From Being to Becoming* (San Francisco: W. E. Freeman, 1980).

after Boltzmann by Planck. Again, as with Darwin, evolution and probability, randomness, are closely related. However, Boltzmann's result is different and even contradictory to that of Darwin. Probability will reach its maximum when *uniformity is achieved*. Think about a system formed by two boxes which may communicate through a small hole. Equilibrium will obviously be achieved when the number of particles in the two boxes is the same. Therefore, the approach to equilibrium corresponds to the destruction of privileged initial conditions, to the forgetting of initial structures, in contrast to Darwin, where evolution means the creation of new structures.

Thus we come to the first question, to the first contradiction which we have inherited from the nineteenth century: *how can Boltzmann and Darwin both be right?* How can we describe both the destruction of structures and processes involving self-organization? Still, as I have already emphasized, both approaches use common elements: the idea of probability (expressed in Boltzmann's theory in terms of the collisions between particles) and irreversibility emerging as a result of this probabilistic description. Before I shall explain how both Boltzmann and Darwin can be right, let us describe the second contradiction which we had to face.

III

The problematics to which we come now lie much deeper than the opposition between Boltzmann and Darwin. The prototype of classical physics is classical mechanics, the study of motion, the *description of trajectories* leading a point from position A to position B. Two of the basic characteristics of the dynamical description are its deterministic and *reversible* character. Once appropriate initial conditions are given, we can predict the trajectory rigorously. Moreover, the direction of time does not play any role: prediction and retro-prediction are identical. Therefore, on the fundamental dynamic level there seems to be no place for randomness or for irreversibility. To some extent the situation remains the same in quantum theory, where we speak of wave function rather than trajectories. Again the wave function evolves according to reversible deterministic law.

Consequently, the universe appears as a vast automaton. We have already mentioned that for Einstein, time in the sense of directed time, of irreversibility, was an illusion. Quite generally, as it appears in innumerable books and publications, the classical attitude in respect to time has been some form of distrust. For example, in his monograph *The Ambidextrous Universe*, Martin Gardner writes that the second law only makes certain processes *improbable*, never impossible. In other words, the law of increase of entropy refers only to a *practical* difficulty without any deep foundation. Similarly, in his classic book *Chance and Necessity*, Jacques Monod expresses the view that life is only an *accident* in the history of nature.[15] It is a kind of fluctuation which for some not very clearly understood reasons is able to maintain itself.

It is certain that, whatever our final apprehension of these complex problems, our universe has a pluralistic, complex character. Structures may disappear, as in a diffusion process, but structures may appear, as in biology and, even more clearly, in social processes. Some phenomena are, so far as we know, well described by deterministic equations, as is the case for planetary motions; but some, like biological evolution, likely involve stochastic processes. Even a scientist convinced of the validity of deterministic descriptions would probably hesitate to imply that at the very moment of the Big Bang the date of this lecture was already inscribed in the laws of nature.

How then to overcome the apparent contradiction between these concepts? We are living in a *single universe*. As we shall see, we begin to appreciate the meaning of these problems; we begin to see that irreversibility, life, are inserted in the basic laws,

[15] *Le Hasard et la nécessité* (Paris: Seuil, 1970), pp. 194–95.

even on the microscopic level. Moreover, the importance which we give to the various phenomena we may observe and describe is quite different from, I would even say opposite to, what was suggested by classical physics. There the basic processes, as I mentioned, were considered *deterministic* and *reversible*. Processes involving randomness or irreversibility were considered to be exceptions, mere artifacts. Today *we see everywhere the role of irreversible processes, of fluctuations.* The models considered by classical physics appear to us now to correspond only to limited situations which we can create artificially, for example by putting matter into a box and waiting for it to reach equilibrium.

The *artificial* may be deterministic and reversible. The *natural* contains essential elements of randomness and irreversibility. This leads to a new view of matter in which matter is no longer passive, as described in the mechanical world view, but is associated with spontaneous activity. This change is so deep that I believe we can really speak about a *new dialogue of man with nature.*

IV

Of course, it has taken many unexpected developments both in theoretical concepts and experimental discoveries to go from the classic description of nature to the new one which is emerging. In brief, we were looking for all-embracing schemes, for symmetries, for immutable general laws, and we have discovered the mutable, the temporal, the complex. Examples abound. As you know, quantum theory predicts a *remarkable symmetry*, the one which should exist between matter and antimatter, but our world does not have this symmetry. Matter dominates greatly over antimatter. This is quite a happy circumstance, as otherwise the annihilation between matter and antimatter would mean the end of all massive particles. The discovery of a large number of *unstable* particles is another example; it may even be that all particles are unstable. Anyway, the idea of an unchanging, permanent substrate for matter has been shattered.

Who could have predicted that (in contrast to the views of Giordano Bruno) the concept of evolution would be applicable to the world as a whole; and, as a matter of fact, astrophysical discoveries, and especially the famous residual black body radiation, leave little doubt that the world as a whole has undergone a remarkable evolution.

How to speak, then, about immutable, eternal laws? We certainly cannot speak about laws of life at a moment when there was no life. The very concept of law which emerged at the time of Descartes and Newton, a time of absolute monarchies, has to be revised.

Of special importance in the context of this lecture are experiments dealing with macroscopic physics, with chemistry — in other words, with nature on our own scale. The classical view (remember our discussion of Boltzmann's interpretation of the second law of thermodynamics) focused its interest on the transition from order to disorder. Now we find everywhere transitions from disorder to order, processes involving *self-organization* of matter. If you had asked a physicist a few years ago what exactly physics explains and what remains open, he might have answered that we obviously do not sufficiently understand elementary particles or cosmological features of the universe as a whole, but in between, our knowledge is pretty satisfactory. Today a growing minority (to which I belong) would not share this optimistic view. I am, on the contrary, convinced that we are only at the beginning of a deeper understanding of the nature around us, and this seems to me of outstanding importance for the embedding of *life in matter as well as of man in life.*

V

We shall now briefly review the way in which the two contradictions which we have mentioned can be approached today. First of all, how can we describe the origin of structures, of self-organization? This problem has been the object of many publications, and I may be quite brief.[16] Once we attach entropy to a physical system, we may distinguish between equilibrium or near equilibrium on one hand and situations corresponding to *far from equilibrium* on the other. What has been shown is that near equilibrium matter indeed conforms to Boltzmann's paradigm; structures are destroyed. If we perturb such a system, the system responds by restoring its initial condition; such systems are therefore stable. In a sense, such systems are always able to develop mechanisms which make them *immune to perturbation*. However, these properties do not extend to far-from-equilibrium conditions. The key words there are *nonlinearity, instability, bifurcation*. In brief, this means that if we drive a system sufficiently far from equilibrium, its state may become unstable in respect to perturbation. The exact point at which this may happen is called the *bifurcation point*. At this point, the old solution becoming unstable, new solutions emerge which may correspond to quite different behavior of matter. A spectacular example is the appearance of chemical clocks in far-from-equilibrium conditions. The experimental demonstration of the existence of chemical clocks is today a routine experiment which is performed in most courses in chemistry at colleges and universities. It is a very simple experiment, and, still, I believe it is perhaps one of the most important experiments of the century. Let me briefly explain why I think so.

In this experiment we have basically two types of molecules. Let us call one species A (the red molecules), the other B (the blue molecules). When we think about some chaotic collisions going on at random, we expect that the interchange between A and B would lead to a uniform color with occasional flashes of red or blue. This is not what happens with appropriate chemicals in far-from-equilibrium conditions. The whole system becomes

---

[16] See, for example, G. Nicolis and I. Prigogine, *Self-Organization in Nonequilibrium Systems* (New York, London, Sydney, Toronto: Wiley Interscience, 1977); also, P. Glansdorff and I. Prigogine, *Thermodynamic Theory of Structure, Stability and Fluctuations* (London, New York, Sydney, Toronto: Wiley Interscience, 1971).

red, then blue, and again red. This shows that molecules may *communicate* over large, macroscopic distances and over macroscopic times. They have means to signal each other their state in order to react together. This is very unexpected behavior indeed. We always thought that molecules interacted only through short-range forces; each molecule would only know its direct neighbors. Here, on the contrary, the system acts as a whole. Such behavior was traditionally associated with biological systems, and here we see it already arising in relatively simple nonliving systems.

A second aspect I want to emphasize is the idea of *symmetry breaking* associated with some of the bifurcations. The equations of reaction and diffusion are highly symmetrical; if we replace the geometric coordinates x, y, z by $-x$, $-y$, $-z$, which corresponds to space inversion, these equations would not change. Still, after bifurcation we may have different solutions, each of which has a broken symmetry. Of course, if we had, say, a "left" solution, we would also have a "right" solution, but it may happen that in nature we observe for some reason only one of the solutions. Everyone has observed that shells often have a preferential chirality. Pasteur went so far as to see in the breaking of symmetry the very characteristic of life. Again we see in nonlife a precursor of this property. Here I want to emphasize that solutions of symmetrical equations may have less symmetry than the equations themselves. This will be an essential point when we discuss the roots of time in nature.

Finally, the appearance of bifurcations in far-from-equilibrium conditions leads to an irreducible stochastic random element on the macroscopic level. Deterministic theories are of no help in permitting us to predict which of the branches arising at the bifurcation point will be followed at the bifurcation point. We have here an example of the essential role of *probability*. You may remember that in quantum mechanics probability already plays an essential role; this is the essence of the famous Heisenberg uncertainty relation. There one could object by saying that we living beings are made of so many elementary particles that quantum effects are being washed out by the laws of large numbers. However, this is no longer possible when we speak about bifurcation of chemical systems far from equilibrium. Here irreducible probabilistic effects appear on our *own level*. Clearly there is a relation with the role of fluctuations and the Darwinian theory of the origin of species. Again you see why I mentioned earlier that in the present perspective life appears much less isolated, as having much deeper roots in the basic laws of nature.

VI

We come now to the second problem, which, I have to tell you immediately, is vastly more difficult. The second law of thermodynamics belongs traditionally to macroscopic physics, but, curiously, its meaning has some elements in common with microscopic theories like quantum theory and relativity. Indeed, all these theoretical constructs have one element in common: they indicate some limit to our manipulation of nature. For example, the existence of the velocity of light as a universal constant indicates that we cannot transmit signals with a speed greater than that of light in a vacuum. Similarly, the existence of the quantum-mechanical constant h, Planck's constant, indicates that we cannot measure simultaneously the momentum and position of an elementary particle. In the same spirit, the second law of thermodynamics indicates that we cannot realize certain types of experiments despite the fact that they are compatible with all other known laws of physics. For example, we cannot drive a thermal engine using the heat of a single heat source, such as the ocean. That is the meaning of the impossibility of a "perpetuum mobile of the second kind."

I believe that this does not mean, however, that physics now becomes a subjectivistic physics, some result of our preferences or convictions, but is indeed a physics subjected to intrinsic constraints that identify us as a part of the physical world we are describing. It is this physics which presupposes an observer situated in the world that is confirmed by experiment. Our dialogue with nature is successful only if carried on from *within* nature.

But how to understand irreversibility, no longer in terms of macroscopic physics, but in terms of the basic laws, be they classical or quantum? I have already mentioned the bold attempt of Boltzmann to relate irreversibility to probability theory. But, in turn, what can probability mean in a world in which particles or wave functions evolve according to deterministic laws? In his beautiful book *Unended Quest*, Popper has described the tragic struggle of Boltzmann and the way in which he was finally obliged to retreat and to admit that there would be no intrinsic arrow of time in nature.[17] Again we come back to Einstein's lapidary conclusion: Time is an illusion.

We can now take up Boltzmann's quest because we have a much better understanding of dynamics, as a result of the work of great mathematicians such as Poincaré, Lyapounov, and, more recently, Kolmogorov.[18] Without their work this problem would still be a question of conjecture. Let us first observe that irreversibility *is not a universal*. We have already mentioned that there are systems, like an isolated spring, for which entropy has no relevance, its motion being entirely reversible. Therefore, we cannot hope that irreversibility may be a property of *all* dynamical systems. What we have to do is to identify dynamical systems of the right complexity, systems for which a formulation of the second law on a microscopic basis becomes possible.

We can of course not go into technical detail here; however, the main point is the recent discovery of *highly unstable dynamical systems*. In such systems the trajectories starting with two points as near to each other as we want diverge exponentially in time. But then the concept of trajectory ceases to be meaningful. We can only reach finite accuracy.

---

[17] K. Popper, *Unended Quest* (La Salle, Ill.: Open Court, 1976).

[18] A. N. Kolmogorov, *La théorie générale des systèmes dynamiques et la mécanique classique*, Amsterdam Congress I (1954), pp. 315–33.

In spite of the fact that we start with deterministic equations, the solutions appear "chaotic." Some authors speak of "deterministic chaos." Curiously, strong probability elements appear in the core of dynamics.

We can only speak of average behavior. Such systems can be called *intrinsically random*. Indeed, as has been shown by my colleagues Misra and Courbage and myself, their behavior is so stochastic that they can be mapped into a probabilistic process called a Markov process, reaching equilibrium either for t → + ∞ in the distant future or t → − ∞ in the distant past.[19]

So we have already justified one of Boltzmann's basic institutions. It is indeed meaningful to speak of probabilities even in the frame of classical mechanics, but *not for all systems, only for highly unstable systems for which the concept of a trajectory loses its meaning*. Now, how can we go further and go from intrinsically random to *intrinsically irreversible* systems?

This requires supplementary conditions. We need representations of dynamics which have less symmetry than the full time-inversion symmetry of the basic equations. For example, in hard spheres, a possible situation is one in which for distant past the velocities of a group of particles were really parallel and for distant future the distribution becomes random as required by equilibrium. The time-inversion symmetry requires that there would also exist a situation in which in the distant past velocities were random and in a distant future they would tend to be parallel. One situation is obtained through the velocity inversion of the other. In fact only the first situation is observed, while the second is not. The second law of thermodynamics on the macroscopic level expresses precisely the exclusion of one of the two situations which are velocity inverses one of the other.

---

[19] B. Misra and I. Prigogine, "Time, Probability and Dynamics," in *Long-Time Prediction in Dynamics*, C. W. Horton, L. E. Reichl, and A. G. Szebehely, eds. (New York: Wiley, 1983). Also see M. Courbage and I. Prigogine, "Intrinsic randomness and intrinsic irreversibility in classical dynamical systems," *Proceedings of the National Academy of Sciences* 80 (1983), pp. 2412–16.

Irreversibility can have a microscopic meaning only if there are representations of dynamics which are not invariable in respect to time inversions, in spite of the fact that the initial equations are.

Let us emphasize the remarkable analogy between such situations and the symmetry-breaking bifurcations we mentioned earlier. There also in some cases we may derive from a symmetrical equation two solutions, one "left," one "right" — each of which taken separately breaks the space symmetry of the equation. We may now make precise what the second law may mean on the microscopic level. It states that only situations which go to equilibrium in the future may be prepared or observed in nature. This means that the second law is an *exclusion principle* which excludes situations in which in the distant past the velocities of colliding spheres would have been distributed uniformly, while in the distant future they would tend to parallel velocities. On the contrary, the situation in which we start in the distant past particles with nearly parallel velocities which are then randomized by collisions is an experiment which we can perform easily.

I have used here *physical* images. But the important point is that the existence of these representations of dynamics with broken time symmetry can be proved rigorously for highly unstable systems.

For such systems we may associate to each initial condition expressed by a distribution function in phase space a number measuring the information necessary to prepare this state. The initial conditions which are excluded are those for which this information would be infinite.[20]

Note also that the entropy principle cannot be derived from dynamics; it appears as a supplementary condition which has to

[20] I. Prigogine and Cl. Georges, "The second law as a selection principle: the microscopic theory of dissipative processes in quantum systems," *Proceedings of the National Academy of Science* 80 (1983), pp. 4590–94. Also see B. Misra and I. Prigogine, "Irreversibility and Nonlocality," *Letters in Mathematical Physics* 7 (1983), pp. 421–29.

be tested experimentally as any other law of physics. The basic point, however, is that this exclusion principle is not contradictory to dynamics, once it is admitted that at a given time it is *propagated* by dynamics.

The probability interpretation of Boltzmann is only possible because there exists this exclusion principle which provides us with an arrow of time.

Irreversibility as in the theory of Darwin, or also as in the theory of Boltzmann, is an even stronger property than randomness. I find this quite natural. Indeed, what could irreversibility mean in a deterministic concept of the universe in which tomorrow is already potentially present today? Irreversibility presupposes a universe in which there are limitations in the prediction of the future. I want again to emphasize that, in the spirit of this explanation, *irreversibility is not a universal property.* However the world as a whole seems to belong to these complex systems, intrinsically random, for which irreversibility is meaningful, and it is to this category of systems with broken time symmetries that all phenomena of life belong and, as a consequence, all human existence.

You may be astonished that I have spoken little about cosmological theories. Certainly the global state of our universe plays an essential role. It provides the nonequilibrium environment which makes the formation of structures possible. However, I do not believe that the existence of the expanding universe and of the initial Big Bang can by themselves provide an explanation of irreversibility. We observe, as already indicated, both reversible and irreversible processes despite the fact that all processes, reversible or not, are embedded in the expanding universe.

VII

The microscopic interpretation of the second law is very recent. I am personally convinced that it will lead to profound changes in our conception of matter. Some preliminary results have been worked out by my colleagues and myself, but what I shall say now is to some extent an anticipation which may or may not be confirmed by later developments.

If we take the second law together with its probabilistic interpretation seriously, we have to associate equilibrium with maximum probability. Now maximum probability in terms of particles means chaotic uncorrelated motion similar to the way the Greek atomists imagined the physical world. Inversely, we may define particles as the units which are uncorrelated and behave in a chaotic way in thermodynamic equilibrium. What is then the effect of nonequilibrium? It is to create *correlations* between these units, to create order out of the chaotic motions arising in the equilibrium state. This description of nature, in which order is generated out of chaos *through nonequilibrium conditions* provided by our cosmological environment, leads to a physics which is quite similar in its spirit to the world of "processes" imagined by Whitehead.[21] It leads to a conception of matter as active, as in a continuous state of becoming. This picture deviates significantly from the classical description of physics, of change in terms of forces or fields. It is a momentous step to leave the royal road opened by Newton, Maxwell, and Einstein. But I believe that the unification of dynamics and thermodynamics paves the way to a radically new description of temporal evolution of physical systems, a description which again, to my mind, is much closer to what we see on the macroscopic level, be it in the nonliving or the living world.

We may quote as examples the highly correlated distribution of nucleotides in the fundamental biological molecules, and perhaps even the distribution of letters which are assembled in words to form our language.

---

[21] A. N. Whitehead, *Process and Reality; An Essay in Cosmology* (New York: Macmillan Co., The Free Press, 1969), p. 20.

VIII

Over all my scientific career, the attitude I have taken has been to consider the law of entropy increase, the second law of thermodynamics, as a basic law of nature. I was following the views Planck expressed in the following text:

> The impracticability of perpetual motion of the second kind is granted, yet its absolute impossibility is contested, since our limited experimental appliances, supposing it were possible, would be insufficient for the realization of the ideal processes which the line of proof presupposes. This position, however, proves untenable. It would be absurd to assume that the validity of the second law depends in any way on the skill of the physicist or chemist in observing or experimenting. The gist of the second law has nothing to do with experiment; the law asserts briefly that *there exists in nature a quantity which changes always in the same sense in all natural processes.* The proposition stated in this general form may be correct or incorrect; but whichever it may be, it will remain so, irrespective of whether thinking and measuring beings exist on the earth or not, and whether or not, assuming they do exist, they are able to measure the details of physical or chemical processes more accurately by one, two, or a hundred decimal places than we can. The limitations to the law, if any, must lie in the same province as its essential idea, in the observed Nature, and not in the Observer. That man's experience is called upon in the deduction of the law is of no consequence; for that is, in fact, our only way of arriving at a knowledge of natural law.[22]

However, Planck's views remained isolated. As we have noticed, most scientists considered the second law to be the result of approximation, or the intrusion of subjective views into the exact laws of physics. Our attitude is the opposite: we have looked for the limits which the second law brings into the world of dynamics.

[22] M. Planck, *Treatise on Thermodynamics* (New York: Dover Publications, 1945), p. 106.

In other words, our goal is to unify dynamics and thermo-dynamics. It is clear that in such a view randomness, fluctuations, and irreversibility will play an essential role at the microscopic level quite different from the marginal role they played in the traditional descriptions of nature. This goal is far from being realized, but on the road we have been led to a series of surprising findings, some of which I have summarized in this lecture.

I remain stunned by the variety of non-equilibrium structures which have been discovered experimentally, some of which we may now describe theoretically. Still, we are only at the level of 'taxonomy'.

We have already mentioned the work of great mathematicians such as Poincaré or Kolmogorov in classical mechanics. As its result, we know that classical dynamics may lead to situations in which the concept of trajectories loses its meaning, and in which we can only make probabilistic statements. Curiously, chemistry is now also going through a comparable reconceptualization. In many instances, we have to go beyond the deterministic approach of chemical kinetics and to take into account fluctuation and randomness, even in systems formed of a large number of molecules. At the microscopic level, irreversibility emerges as symmetry-breaking in systems reaching a sufficient degree of randomness.

The second law limits what is observable. It appears as an exclusion principle propagated by classical or quantum mechanics.

Perhaps the most unexpected aspect is that at all levels order, coherence, emerges from chaos for non-equilibrium conditions: An equilibrium world would be chaotic; the non-equilibrium world achieves a degree of coherence which, at least for me, is a source of surprise.

IX

In this lecture I have discussed some steps in the rediscovery of time in the physical sciences. We have seen that time in the sense of duration, of irreversibility, is basically related to the role of randomness, in full accord with the genial intuition of Boltzmann.

Since the discovery of quantum mechanics, in which probability plays an essential role, the meaning of randomness has led to many controversies. It appears today that deterministic schemes which make predictions valid in each individual case are inaccessible to us in a wide range of phenomena from microscopic physics up to the level of molecules and of life. Of course this situation may change, but we see no sign for such a change to occur over the next years.

In this context let us emphasize that we don't know how to describe reality as it would appear to an observer who in some sense would be situated outside this world. We can only deal with the problems of determinism or randomness as they are included in the schemes we formulate to describe our experience with the world and us.

One is reminded of the dialogue between Einstein and Tagore.[23] In this most interesting dialogue on the nature of reality Einstein was emphasizing that science has to be independent of the existence of any observer. As I mentioned at the beginning of this lecture, his realism led him to paradoxes. Time and therefore human existence become illusions. To the contrary, Tagore emphasized that even if absolute truth could have a meaning it would be inaccessible to the human mind. I found this dialogue so interesting that I have reproduced it as an appendix to this paper.

The controversy between Einstein and Tagore is only meaningful if man is supposed to be separated from nature. If the imbedding of man in nature is taken into account, human truths become truths of nature. Curiously enough, the present evolution of science goes in the direction stated by the great Indian poet. Whatever we call reality, it is only open to us through constructs

---

[23] R. Tagore, "The Nature of Reality," *Modern Review* XLIX (Calcutta 1931), pp. 42–43.

of our minds. This has been concisely expressed by D. S. Kothari: "The simple fact is that no measurement, no experiment or observation is possible without a relevant theoretical framework." [24]

In a more sophisticated form this phenomenon appears in quantum theory through the intervention of "operators" which are associated with physical quantities.

The problems of the limits of determinism, randomness, irreversibility and the notion of reality are closely connected, and we begin to see their relations.

As we are able to find the roots of time in nature, time ceases to be the concept which separates men from nature. It now expresses our belonging to nature, not our alienation.

The visions of the world around us and of the world in us converge. As I deliver this lecture in Delhi, why not stress that this type of convergence, of synthesis of the external world around us and the internal world inside us, is one of the recurrent themes of Indian philosophy.

We now overcome the temptation to reject time as an illusion. Far from that, we are back to Valéry's anticipation: "Durée est construction, vie est construction." [25] In a universe in which tomorrow is not contained in today, time is to be constructed. Valéry's sentence expresses our responsibility in this construction of the future — not only *our* future, but the future of mankind. With this conclusion the problem of human values, of ethics, even of art takes a new form. We may now see music with its elements of expectation, of improvisation, with its arrow of time as an allegory of becoming, of physics in its etymological Greek sense.

The dialectic between what is *in* time and what is *out* time, between external truths and time-oriented existence, will probably continue forever.

[24] D. S. Kothari, *Some Thoughts on Truth*, Anniversary Address, Indian National Science Academy, Bahadur Shah Zafar Marg, New Delhi, 1975, p. 5.

[25] Paul Valéry, *Oeuvres* II, Bibliothèque de la Pléiade (Paris: Editions Gallimard, 1960), p. 768.

But perhaps we are now in a privileged moment where we begin to perceive a little better the junction, the passage between stillness and motion, time arrested and time passing.

It is this moment with its incertitudes, its open questions, but also its hopes for a more integrated human world which I have tried to describe in this lecture.

APPENDIX

THE NATURE OF REALITY

A conversation between Rabindranath Tagore and Albert Einstein on the afternoon of July 14, 1930, at Professor Einstein's residence in Kaputh, published in the Modern Review XLIX *(1931), Calcutta.*

E: Do you believe in the Divine as isolated from the world?

T: Not isolated. The infinite personality of Man comprehends the Universe. There cannot be anything that cannot be subsumed by the human personality, and this proves that the truth of the Universe is human truth.

I have taken a scientific fact to explain this. Matter is composed of protons and electrons, with gaps between them, but matter may seem to be solid without the links in spaces which unify the individual electrons and protons. Similarly humanity is composed of individuals, yet they have their inter-connection of human relationship, which gives living unity to man's world. The entire universe is linked up with us, as individuals, in a similar manner; it is a human universe.

I have pursued this thought through art, literature, and the religious consciousness of man.

E: There are two different conceptions about the nature of the Universe:

1. The world as a unity dependent on humanity.

2. The world as a reality independent of the human factor.

T: When our universe is in harmony with man, the eternal, we know it as truth, we feel it as beauty.

E: This is the purely human conception of the universe.

T: There can be no other conception. This world is a human world — the scientific view of it is also that of the scientific man. Therefore, the world apart from us does not exist; it is a relative world, depending for its reality upon our consciousness. There is some standard of reason and enjoyment which gives it truth, the standard of the Eternal Man whose experiences are through our experiences.

E: This is a realization of the human entity.

T: Yes, one eternal entity. We have to realize it through our emotions and activities. We realized the Supreme Man who has no individual limitations through our limitations. Science is concerned with that which is not confined to individuals; it is the impersonal human world of truths. Religion realizes these truths and links them up with our deeper needs; our individual consciousness of truth gains universal significance. Religion applies values to truth, and we know truth as good through our own harmony with it.

E: Truth, then, or Beauty is not independent of Man?

T: No.

E: If there were no human beings any more, the Apollo of Belvedere would no longer be beautiful.

T: No!

E: I agree with regard to this conception of Beauty, but not with regard to Truth.

T: Why not? Truth is realized through man.

E: I cannot prove that my conception is right, but that is my religion.

T: Beauty is in the ideal of perfect harmony which is in the Universal Being, Truth the perfect comprehension of the Universal mind. We individuals approach it through our own mistakes and blunders, through our accumulated experiences, through our illumined consciousness — how, otherwise, can we know Truth?

E: I cannot prove that scientific truth must be conceived as a truth that is valid independent of humanity; but I believe it firmly.

I believe, for instance, that the Pythagorean theorem in geometry states something that is approximately true, independent of the existence of man. Anyway, if there is a *reality* independent of man, there is also a truth relative to this reality; and in the same way the negation of the first engenders a negation of the existence of the latter.

T: Truth, which is one with the Universal Being, must essentially be human; otherwise whatever we individuals realize as true can never be called truth, at least the truth which is described as scientific and which only can be reached through the process of logic, in other words, by an organ of thought which is human. According to Indian philosophy there is Brahman, the absolute Truth which cannot be conceived by the isolation of the individual mind or described by words but can only be realized by completely merging the individual in its infinity. But such a truth cannot belong to Science. The nature of truth which we are discussing is an appearance, that is to say, what appears to be true to the human mind and therefore is human, and may be called *Maya* or illusion.

E: So according to your conception, which may be the Indian conception, it is not the illusion of the individual but of humanity as a whole.

T: In science we go through the discipline of eliminating the personal limitations of our individual minds and thus reach that comprehension of truth which is in the mind of the Universal Man.

E: The problem begins whether Truth is independent of our consciousness.

T: What we call truth lies in the rational harmony between the subjective and objective aspects of reality, both of which belong to the super-personal man.

E: Even in our everyday life, we feel compelled to ascribe a reality independent of man to the objects we use. We do this to connect the experiences of our senses in a reasonable way. For instance, if nobody is in this house, yet that table remains where it is.

T: Yes, it remains outside the individual mind but not the universal mind. The table which I perceive is perceptible by the same kind of consciousness which I possess.

E: Our natural point of view in regard to the existence of truth apart from humanity cannot be explained or proved, but it is a belief which nobody can lack — no primitive beings even. We attribute to Truth a super-human objectivity; it is indispensable to us, this reality which is independent of our existence and our experience and our mind — though we cannot say what it means.

T: Science has proved that the table as a solid object is an appearance and therefore that which the human mind perceives as a table would not exist if that mind were naught. At the same time it must be admitted that the fact that the ultimate physical reality of the table is nothing but a multitude of separate revolving centres of electric force also belongs to the human mind.

In the apprehension of truth there is an eternal conflict between the universal human mind and the same mind confined in the individual. The perpetual process of reconciliation is being carried on in our science, philosophy, in our ethics. In any case, if there be any truth absolutely unrelated to humanity, then for us it is absolutely non-existing.

It is not difficult to imagine a mind to which sequence of things happens not in space but only in time, like the sequence of notes in music. For such a mind its conception of reality is akin to the musical reality in which Pythagorean geometry can have no meaning. There is the reality of paper, infinitely different from the reality of literature. For the kind of mind possessed by the moth which eats that paper literature is absolutely non-existent, yet for Man's mind literature has a greater value of truth than the paper itself. In a similar manner, if there be some truth which has no sensuous or rational relation to human mind, it will ever remain as nothing so long as we remain human beings.

E: Then I am more religious than you are!

T: My religion is in the reconciliation of the super-personal man, the Universal human spirit, in my own individual being. This was the subject of my Hibbert Lectures, which I called "The Religion of Man."

The Incompleat Egoist

DAVID GAUTHIER

THE TANNER LECTURES ON HUMAN VALUES

Delivered at
Stanford University

May 10, 1983

DAVID GAUTHIER is a native Torontonian now resident in Pittsburgh. He was educated at the University of Toronto, Harvard University, and the University of Oxford. From 1958 to 1980 he was a member of the Department of Philosophy at the University of Toronto, rising from Lecturer through the ranks to Professor and becoming Chairman in 1974. He is now Professor of Philosophy, Senior Fellow in the Center for Philosophy of Science, and Chairman of the Department of Philosophy at the University of Pittsburgh. In 1979 he was elected a Fellow of the Royal Society of Canada.

Professor Gauthier is the author of two books, editor of a third, and is currently completing a fourth, "Morals by Agreement," which brings to fruition almost twenty years' work in developing a contractarian theory of morality. He has also written numerous papers, mainly in moral and political theory. The most enduring of his non-philosophical interests is in light rail transit.

I. WHAT CAN AN EGOIST DO?

1. "Egoism . . . is the doctrine which holds that we ought each of us to pursue our own greatest happiness as our ultimate end." [1] Thus G. E. Moore, who proceeded to charge this doctrine with "flagrant contradiction." [2] "The egoistic principle," Brian Medlin asserted, "is inconsistent." [3] In levelling these accusations, Moore and Medlin have been representative of a host of philosophers who have found egoism wanting in rationality. But why accuse the egoist? Left to himself, surely he seeks only to do as well for himself as possible, and this intent, if not wholly attractive, seems to fall squarely within the confines of the economist's utility-maximizing conception of practical rationality — hardly, then, what we should expect to find contradictory or inconsistent.[4] Philosophers are blessed with both talent for and desire of finding paradox where other mortals suspect none, yet what, *rationally*, could be at fault with the attempt to do as well for oneself as possible?

As a philosopher, I have up my sleeve what, if not truly paradoxical, should seem unexpectedly puzzling. But the questions I shall raise about egoism come, not from the traditional philosophical repertoire, but rather from the theory of rational choice.

---

[1] G. E. Moore, *Principia Ethica* (Cambridge: At the University Press, 1903), p. 96.

[2] Ibid., p. 102.

[3] Brian Medlin, "Ultimate Principles and Ethical Egoism," *Australasian Journal of Philosophy* 35 (1957), p. 118.

[4] Note that the egoist's aim is not dictated by the utility-maximizing conception of practical rationality. What is rational, according to this conception, is to do as well as possible — to maximize some measure defined over the possible outcomes of one's actions. The characteristics of the measure to be maximized are left largely unspecified by this maximizing requirement. The egoist adds to the idea of doing as well as possible the specification that the measure be self-directed, so that he do as well *for himself* as possible.

More particularly, although the lone egoist will pass rational scrutiny, yet when put with others of his persuasion, in interaction in which each seeks to maximize his own happiness, grounds for challenging the rationality of egoism appear. And these grounds concern, not so much the egoist's concern with his own happiness, but rather his maximizing principle of choice. Something is amiss in our account of practical rationality.

2. Let us then focus briefly on the theory of rational choice. We may first recall a dictum laid down by John Rawls: "The theory of justice is a part, perhaps the most significant part, of the theory of rational choice." [5] I shall interpret this dictum in a quite un-Rawlsian way, and in order to sketch my interpretation I must temporarily set egoism to one side; but before doing this, let us note an immediate connection between Rawls' claim and our concern with the rationality of egoism. If the theory of justice is literally a part of the theory of rational choice, and so much a part that justice proves to be required in rational choice, then it would seem that either justice is compatible with egoism, or that egoism is not compatible with rationality. If the former is implausible, then we may expect the case for the rationality of justice to be linked to the case against egoism. And both will depend on a proper understanding of rational choice.

Before concluding our reflections we shall indeed have proceeded from an argument against the rationality of egoism to an argument linking, not only justice, but morality, with rational choice. But that link comes at the end of a long chain. Here let us reflect on what Rawls said and generalize it to what I believe — that moral theory as a whole is part of choice or decision theory. What I believe, however, is *not* what Rawls believes.

I treat moral principles as principles *for* rational choice. In a very general and important type of interaction, which I shall call *cooperative*, a rational actor would — I claim — base his or her

[5] John Rawls, *A Theory of Justice* (Cambridge: Harvard University Press, 1972), p. 16.

choice among possible actions on a moral principle, provided he or she expected others to do likewise. In section five of this part I shall consider what a principle for choice, or for action, is, and in the second part I shall explain why a rational actor would base choices on principles appropriately characterized as moral.

Rawls treats the principles of justice, not as principles *for* rational choice, but as objects *of* rational choice.[6] This is a very different matter. For Rawls the principles of justice determine the basic structure of society. He asks, what principles, constitutive of society, would a rational individual choose in the "original position," behind a veil of ignorance making him unaware of his identity except as a free and equal person. Rawls identifies the principles so chosen with the principles of justice. This is how he connects the theory of justice with the theory of rational choice.

Note the differences between us. Rawls asks: *what* would rational actors choose behind a veil of ignorance? He answers: they would choose the principles of justice. I ask: *how* would rational actors choose in cooperative interaction? I answer: they would choose on the basis of moral principles. For Rawls the principles of justice constitute the *solution* to a particular problem of rational choice.[7] For me moral principles are used by persons in *solving* certain problems of rational choice. Rawls uses principles of rational choice as tools in developing his theory of justice. I develop moral theory as part of the theory of rational choice — as part of the theory that determines what principles a rational actor would use in choice.

There is a second equally important difference between Rawls' attempt to use rational choice in characterizing justice and my attempt to develop morality as part of rational choice. And this difference bears directly on my concern with egoism. The theory of rational choice examines two significantly different forms of

---

[6] My account here reflects sections 2–4, of *A Theory of Justice.*

[7] See *A Theory of Justice*, section 20.

agency, parametric and strategic.[8] The parametric actor chooses in an environment that, whether its characteristics be known to him or not, he treats as fixed in relation to his choice. His choice is a response to circumstances that are not, or are not considered to be, responsive to him as choosing. The strategic actor chooses in an environment that is responsive to him as a chooser. He relates his choices to an environment that includes other actors seeking to relate to his choices. Egoism, we shall find, succeeds for parametric choice but fails for strategic choice.

To illuminate the difference between parametric and strategic choice, consider a simple illustration. Jane must choose whether to go to Ann's party. She wants to go, but only if Brian will not be there. In case one, Jane expects Brian to go to Ann's party unless his father needs him to deliver pizza, a matter having nothing to do with Jane. Whether Brian is needed to deliver pizza is, for Jane, an unknown but fixed circumstance. If she considers it likely that he is needed, she will choose to go to Ann's party; if she considers it unlikely, she will choose not to go. Jane faces a problem of parametric choice.

In case two, Brian must also choose whether to go to Ann's party. He does not want to go unless Jane will be there. Here Jane chooses on the basis of her expectation of Brian's choice, and Brian chooses on the basis of his expectation of Jane's choice. Thus Jane chooses on the basis of her expectation of a choice based on an expectation of her choice. And Brian chooses similarly. Each faces a problem of strategic choice.

Rawls relates the principles of justice, not to strategic, but to parametric choice. This may seem surprising, since he supposes that the principles would be agreed to by all rational persons in the original position. And so it may seem that each seeks to relate his choice of principles to the choices of others who are them-

---

[8] For this distinction between parametric and strategic, see Jon Elster, *Ulysses and the Sirens: Studies in Rationality and Irrationality* (Cambridge: Cambridge University Press, 1979), pp. 18–19, 117–23.

selves seeking to relate their choices to his choice. But Rawls emphasizes that this appearance of strategic interaction is misleading.[9] Behind the veil of ignorance, persons are identically situated, not only in their objective circumstances but also subjectively, in that each is completely ignorant of his capacities and interests and so is unable to distinguish himself from his fellows. They have, then, no basis for bargaining with one another, and agreement on the principles of justice may be represented by the choice of a single representative individual. The problem of rational choice to be solved is therefore one of individual decision under extraordinary uncertainty. And this is a problem of parametric choice.

I relate moral principles to strategic choice. As I shall argue, moral principles direct choice in cooperative interaction in which each person, fully aware of his or her particular circumstances, capacities, and concerns, seeks to relate his or her actions to those of others in ways beneficial to each. The rationale for moral principles — and the irrationale, we may say, for egoistic principles — emerges from an examination of the structure of such interaction.

At the end of our enquiry I shall return to this difference between Rawls and myself — a difference that also distinguishes my contractarian approach to moral theory from the utilitarian argument of John Harsanyi.[10] I suggest that there is a deep incoherence in the attempt to relate moral principles to parametric choice, since parametric choice does not fully accommodate the interaction of rational beings. Strategic rationality, which focusses on this interaction, is not fully egoistic, and moral theory is properly based on the failure of strategic egoism.

3. Once again I have indicated a destination. At the end of our brief journey we should understand more clearly both why

---

[9] See *A Theory of Justice*, p. 139.

[10] See John C. Harsanyi, *Essays on Ethics, Social Behavior, and Scientific Explanation* (Dordrecht and Boston: Reidel, 1976), especially ch. II and ch. VI, sections 1–5.

egoism fails and how morality relates to strategic choice. At the beginning we must relate egoism to parametric rationality.

I shall assume that rational parametric choice may be represented by a simple maximizing model. That is, I shall suppose that a parametrically rational actor behaves as if he is maximizing the expected value of some function defined over the possible outcomes of his choices. For the model adequately to represent risky and uncertain choices, in which the actor does not know the outcome of each possible choice but rather is able to assign to each only a probability distribution over possible outcomes,[11] the function must be uniquely defined up to a positive linear transformation, so that it affords an interval measure of the outcomes. A familiar example of an interval measure is temperature; the zero-point and the unit may be selected arbitrarily, but once selected the unit is constant.

I shall not ask whether rationality in parametric choice is fully captured by maximization. For our purposes we need not decide whether an actor is rational insofar as he maximizes, without consideration of what he maximizes. Thus I shall take maximization only as necessary for parametric rationality. But I shall make one further, crucial assumption — that the value maximized by an actor is relative to him or her. If Mary voted for Reagan and Harry for Carter, then we may suppose that Reagan being President had greater expected value than Carter being President as an object of Mary's choice, but lesser expected value as an object of Harry's choice.

This assumption, that value is relative and that choice is based on actor-relative value, may be related to strategic as well as to parametric rationality. Although we shall find that rational strategic choice may not always be represented by a simple maximizing model, yet strategically rational actors may be considered as assigning values to the possible outcomes. In interaction the in-

---

[11] We speak of risk if the probabilities are objective, of uncertainty if they are subjective.

terval measures defined by the several actors over possible outcomes are logically independent one from another. Brian's most
valued outcome may be, and indeed is, Jane's least valued outcome. An outcome has no single value but a set of values, one for
each actor, or indeed for each person affected by it, and there is no
relationship a priori among the members of the set.

The egoist, whom we kept in a secondary role in our discussion of rational choice, has now reappeared, slightly disguised, as
a species of parametrically rational actor. We first introduced the
egoist as the person who pursues his own greatest happiness. He
is a maximizer, albeit of a rather specific quantity — his own happiness. But for our purposes we may generalize from this characterization and think of the egoist as maximizing whatever actor-
relative value he pleases — perhaps his own happiness, perhaps
not. He is then simply the person whose interests, whatever they
may be, have no necessary link with the interests of his fellows,
so that his values provide a measure of states of affairs quite independent of their values. This generic account affords a very weak
characterization of an egoist, and indeed even an excessively weak
one, since it admits to the egoistic ranks persons whose interests
are other-directed, provided only that their other-directed interests
are not simply dependent on others' interests. But it is all that our
argument will require. Our egoist then is simply a maximizer, or
would-be maximizer, of actor-relative value. He satisfies the necessary condition of parametric rationality.

Before proceeding to face the egoist with the problems of interaction, I should note, out of fairness to G. E. Moore, that in
introducing the maximization of actor-relative value I have already embraced what to him was the contradictory feature of
egoism. For Moore, "The *good* of [something] can in no possible sense be 'private' or belong to me; any more than a thing
can *exist* privately or *for* one person only." [12] Moore could allow

---

[12] *Principia Ethica*, p. 99.

that a state of affairs might further the well-being of one person but not that of another. He could allow that a state of affairs might be good in that it furthered one person's well-being and bad in that it hindered another's. But he denied that a state of affairs could be good in relation to the person whose well-being it furthered and bad in relation to the person whose well-being it hindered. Rather he insisted that it must be good absolutely insofar as it hindered one person's well-being and bad absolutely insofar as it hindered another's.

Moore's position might be formulated as a claim about the universality of reasons for choosing or acting. On this view, for any states of affairs P and Q, if there is a person X who is able to choose between P and Q and has a reason for choosing P over Q, then any person Y able to choose between P and Q has a reason for choosing P over Q. This position is embraced by many philosophers other than Moore, such as R. M. Hare and Thomas Nagel, but in embracing actor-relative value I propose to ignore it.[13]

On my view reasons for choosing have only a weaker universality. For any states of affairs P and Q, if there is a person X who is able to choose between P and Q and has a reason for choosing P over Q, then there is some relation R holding among X, P, and Q, such that, for any person Y who is able to choose between P and Q, (i) R need not hold among Y, P, and Q, but (ii) if R does hold among Y, P, and Q, then Y has a reason for choosing P over Q. The actor-relativity of reasons is assured by founding them on a relation between the actor and the objects of choice that does not hold for every person by virtue of holding for some person.

Suppose that Moore and I agree that enhancing my prospects of survival is a reason for me to choose to have a site for the dis-

---

[13] For Hare, see *Moral Thinking* (Oxford: Clarendon Press, 1981), especially chs. 5–7. For Nagel, see *The Possibility of Altruism* (Oxford: Clarendon Press, 1970), especially ch. X.

posal of nuclear wastes located in the Antarctic rather than in Allegheny County. We might expect that for Moore this would instantiate the claim: for all persons X, Y and all states of affairs P, Q, if P affords X greater survival prospects than Q, Y has a reason for choosing P over Q. For me it instantiates the claim: for all persons X and states of affairs P, Q, if P affords X greater survival prospects than Q, then X has a reason for choosing P over Q.

If Moore were right, and reasons were not actor-relative, then the maximization of some actor-relative measure of possible outcomes would be an irrational basis for choice. Not only egoism, but the entire edifice of the standard theory of rational choice, the theory that characterizes parametric rationality, would collapse. This affords an easy, but in my view unpersuasive, refutation of egoism. In granting actor-relative value, I concede egoism the initial stage of the argument concerning its rationality.

4. We are now ready to ask: what happens when the egoist, or more generally the parametrically rational actor, finds himself interacting with others of his kind? Does the endeavour to maximize actor-relative value involve him in contradiction? Or inconsistency? Or some other form of irrationality? Is it always possible for him to put his egoism into practice? And if, or when, it is possible, is it always rational, or at least not irrational, for him to maximize?

In answering, or trying to answer, these questions, we must focus, not on interaction in general, but on strategic interaction. Were the egoist not faced with strategic problems, problems in which he seeks to adapt his choice to the choices of others adapting their choices to his, the issues we shall raise would not appear. To the extent to which interaction is not conceived in strategic terms, egoism seems fully, and perhaps even paradigmatically, rational.

This is an historically important consideration. For the most thoroughly studied form of interaction, that which occurs in the perfectly competitive market, is parametric and not strategic in character. Although each actor in the market is interacting with others of his kind, yet each chooses in a fixed environment. The firm seeks to maximize profits given known costs of factor supply and known prices reflecting aggregate consumer demand. The consumer seeks to maximize the value of his commodity bundle given known commodity prices. Since choices have fixed and indeed known outcomes, market interaction may be represented by a model that dispenses with interval measures of those outcomes in favour of weak orderings. A world conforming in every detail to the ideal of the perfectly competitive market would not raise the problems that we shall examine. Egoism is rational within the framework of the market, as Adam Smith implicitly recognized in his doctrine of the Invisible Hand, and the modern appeal of egoism is not unrelated to the dominance of the market framework in our practical thought.

But not all economic behaviour is perfectly competitive, and not all behaviour is economic. The market adequately models only a limited range of interaction. In adopting the title *Theory of Games and Economic Behavior*, Von Neumann and Morgenstern were calling attention to the insufficiently understood strategic dimension found in most interaction.[14] And it is this dimension that interests us, as we examine the problems that arise in attempting to extend the simple maximizing model of parametric rationality to accommodate strategic choice.

We shall discover two principal and distinct issues. The first is expressed in the claim that egoism is *inconsistent* — or unable always to give consistent guidance to choice. The second is expressed in the claim that egoism is *self-defeating* — that egoists fall farther short of their objectives than do some non-egoists. The first charge, we shall find, has no simple resolution. The second

---

[14] John Von Neumann and Oskar Morgenstern, *Theory of Games and Economic Behavior* (Princeton: Princeton University Press, 1944), is the seminal work from which studies of strategic rationality have developed.

charge will be sustained, and in sustaining it we shall come to the constructive problem to which our argument is propaedeutic — to the development of moral theory as part of rational choice. We shall then understand why the strategically rational actor must be, or at least must become, a moral actor.

Let us now illustrate the two charges that we shall assess. I shall then spend the remainder of this part in examining inconsistency, leaving self-defeatingness to its successor.

The claim that egoism is inconsistent may be illustrated by our original example of strategic choice. Jane and Brian must each choose whether to go to Ann's party. Each, we suppose, has two and only two choices — to go, or not to go. If both choose to go, then Jane has chosen wrongly; she wants to go to the party, but only if Brian is not there. If neither chooses to go to the party, then Jane has also chosen wrongly; she wants to go to the party if Brian is not there. If one chooses to go and the other chooses not to go, then Brian has chosen wrongly; he wants to go to the party if and only if Jane is there. Whatever Jane and Brian choose, one of them fails to maximize his or her value. Hence one has failed to satisfy the requirements of egoism. But this failure is unavoidable. The requirements, then, can not always be satisfied. Egoism, and indeed the maximization of actor-relative value, is inconsistent.

The claim that egoism is self-defeating may be illustrated by an example long familiar among game theorists and now widely known to philosophers — the Prisoners' Dilemma. Jack and Zack are prisoners charged with a serious crime; each must choose between a confession that implicates the other and non-confession. If only one confesses, he is rewarded for turning state's evidence with a light sentence, while the other receives the maximum. If both confess, each receives a heavy sentence, but short of the maximum. If neither confesses, each will be convicted on a lesser charge and receive a sentence slightly heavier than that which would reward turning state's evidence. Jack reasons that, if Zack confesses, then he avoids the maximum sentence by confessing himself, whereas if Zack does not confess, then he gains the lightest sentence by confessing. Whatever Zack does, Jack does better to confess. Zack of course reasons in a parallel way. Given that neither is able to affect the other's choice by his own, each does better to confess, whatever the other may choose to do. Jack and Zack each maximizes his value by confessing. Each receives a heavy sentence. If neither had confessed, each would have received a lighter sentence. Jack and Zack have both satisfied the requirements of egoism and have reached a mutually costly outcome. The requirements, then, should not always be satisfied. Egoism is self-defeating.

5. To charge egoism with both inconsistency and self-defeatingness may seem excessive. If egoism fails in that it makes demands that can not be met, then why consider whether those demands are also self-defeating? The answer, of course, is that the charge of inconsistency does not affect every situation in which persons may endeavour to act egoistically. Only in some interactions, such as that of Jane and Brian, does egoism fail to direct choice.

We must be clear about the nature of this failure. Either Jane or Brian does not realize her or his most preferred outcome, but this is not sufficient to show failure of choice. If Brian chooses to go to Ann's party, then Jane, whatever she chooses, can not realize her most preferred outcome, which is to be at the party without Brian. If Jane chooses to stay home, then Brian, whatever he chooses, can not realize his most preferred outcome. In these cases, one person's most preferred outcome is excluded by the other's choice. Failure to realize one's most preferred outcome thus need not show that one has chosen wrongly, and does not in itself raise a problem for egoism. Some persons may take egoism to be inconsistent because egoists have incompatible objectives, so that not all can succeed. But the mere existence of incompatible objectives does not prevent any individual from doing as well for himself as possible, where what is possible must be determined in part by the choices of others. However, in the situation we are examining, either Jane or Brian fails to do as well as possible given the other's choice, and it is this failure, to choose what will maximize one's value given the possibilities left open by the choices of others, that is at the root of the charge that egoism is unable always to give consistent directives.

The inconsistency of egoism thus seems to arise in the following way. The egoist would be a maximizer of actor-relative value in strategic interaction. What is required for one to be such a maximizer? It would seem that one must always choose what maximizes one's value given the choices of the others. Our example shows that it may be impossible for everyone to make such a choice. *Any* person can make such a choice; given the choices of others any person has a maximizing alternative. But not *every* person can make such a choice. Not everyone can always be a maximizer of actor-relative value in strategic interaction. Egoism, in requiring this, is inconsistent.

This argument moves too quickly. In a world of risk and uncertainty, even the parametrically rational actor can not ensure that he maximizes actor-relative value. Given his estimate of the probability of alternative circumstances, he can maximize *expected* actor-relative value, but in choice he can set his sights no higher. Similarly, the strategically rational actor must be satisfied if he maximizes expected value. And to do this, he need not always choose what maximizes his value given the choices of the others, but only what maximizes his value given the choices he expects the others to make. If Jane supposes it unlikely that Brian will choose to go to the party, then she may maximize her expected value by choosing to go. If Brian supposes it likely that Jane will choose to go to the party, then he may maximize his expected value by choosing to go. Jane will then be disappointed by the outcome, but her choice, it may seem, satisfies the requirements of egoism. We have found no reason to claim that not everyone can be a maximizer of expected actor-relative value in strategic choice, even if some must be disappointed by the outcome.

But this rejoinder also moves too quickly. Let us suppose that Jane and Brian know each other to be would-be maximizers of actor-relative value. Then for each to maximize expected value, each must choose on an expectation about the choice the other will make based on an expectation about what his or her own choice will be. If Jane chooses to go to the party, she does so expecting Brian to choose not to go because he expects her to choose not to go. If Jane chooses to stay home, she does so expecting Brian to choose to go because he expects her to choose to go. Whatever she chooses, Jane must base her choice, if it maximizes her expected value, on an expectation that requires Brian to have a mistaken expectation about her choice. And similarly, Brian must base his choice on an expectation that requires Jane to have a mistaken expectation about his choice.

We may now give a more satisfactory explanation of the failure that seems to make egoism inconsistent. The egoist would maximize expected actor-relative value in strategic choice. Thus he must seek to maximize his value given the choices he expects to be made by others who seek to maximize their values given the choices they expect to be made by others, himself included. But the following three propositions can not all be true:

1. An egoist always chooses to maximize value given the choices he expects others to make.

2. An egoist always expects other egoists to choose to maximize value given the choices they expect others, himself included, to make.

3. In satisfying 1 and 2, an egoist is never required to suppose that the expectations of other egoists are mistaken.

The failure of egoism thus lies in the necessity of attributing mistaken expectations to others in situations such as that of Jane and Brian, in order to suppose that each person chooses to maximize actor-relative value given the choices he expects the others to make.

Let us introduce some useful terminology for expressing what we have argued. An action maximizing the actor's value in interaction with others is a *best response* to the others' actions. An egoist chooses an expected best response. In some situations no set of actions, one for each person, is a set each member of which is a best response to the other members. In the terminology of the theory of games, a set of mutual best responses is a *Nash-equilibrium* set;[15] in some situations there is no Nash-equilibrium set of actions. In such situations egoists can all choose expected best responses only if some have mistaken expectations. The existence of a Nash-equilibrium set of actions is a necessary condition for successful and informed egoistic choice.

Let us treat a *principle for choice* as a function that takes sets of alternative actions into subsets of themselves. (For any set S, the corresponding subset is then termed the *choice set*, $C(S)$.) A principle is *complete* for any domain if and only if it takes each member of the domain into a non-empty subset. A principle is *egoistic* only if it takes each set S into a subset $C(S)$, the members of which maximize some measure defined over S. In a community of sufficiently informed egoists, a principle that determines a choice for each person involved in an interaction must determine choices that maximize each person's value given the other choices it determines. In other words, a principle that includes in its domain all of the sets of alternative actions making up an interaction must take each set into a subset which has as members only actions belonging also to Nash-equilibrium sets for the interaction. Since for some interactions there is no Nash-equilibrium set, there can be no egoistic principle for choice defined over the domain consisting of all sets of alternative actions in all possible interactions. There can be no egoistic principle of choice complete for all strategic interaction. This gives precise sense to the accusation that egoism is inconsistent.

---

[15] The term "Nash-equilibrium" refers to John F. Nash, who is responsible for the core result concerning equilibrium in strategic interaction to be discussed in the next section.

6. Having called the resources of the theory of rational choice to our aid, we now find that they open unexpected complexities in our attempt to assess the consistency of egoism. Only the first round of our discussion is completed; we begin the second round by turning from *actions* to *strategies*. A strategy is a lottery or probability distribution over possible actions. To this point we have thought of each actor choosing among possible actions; let us now enlarge the choice space and think of each actor choosing among possible strategies. To choose an action is in effect to choose a strategy assigning that action a probability 1 and each alternative a probability 0. Such a strategy is termed *pure*. But there are countless *mixed* strategies which assign a positive probability to each of two or more alternative actions.

We have supposed that each actor may be represented as seeking to maximize the value or expected value of a function that provides an interval measure of possible outcomes. The value assigned to each *action* is the weighted sum of the values of its possible outcomes, where each weight represents the probability of the outcome given performance of the action. The value assigned to each *strategy* is then the weighted sum of the values of its possible actions, where each weight represents the probability assigned to the action by the particular strategy. We now suppose that the egoist seeks to maximize some actor-relative value in choosing among his possible strategies.

With this supposition we may, surprising as it might seem, rescue the egoist from the charge of embracing an inconsistent basis of choice. For more than thirty years ago John F. Nash proved that, in any interaction among finitely many persons, each with only finitely many actions or pure strategies, there is at least one Nash-equilibrium set of strategies.[16] Or in other words, there is at least one set of strategies, one for each actor, each of which is a best response to the other members of the set. And the exis-

---

[16] See John F. Nash, "Noncooperative Games," *Annals of Mathematics* 54 (1951), pp. 286–95.

tence of such a Nash-equilibrium set satisfies our requirement for egoistic choice that is both maximizing and correctly informed.

If we would apply the existence of a Nash-equilibrium set of strategies to resolve the problem of choice facing Jane and Brian, we must provide each with an interval measure of possible outcomes. Rather than doing this and solving the resulting mathematical problem, we shall develop intuitively the idea of determining a pair of strategies each of which is a best response to the other. Suppose that Jane despairs of concealing her strategy choice from Brian. She expects that, should she select a strategy giving a high probability to going to Ann's party, Brian will respond by choosing to go to the party so that the likely outcome will be undesirable for her. And she expects that, should she select a strategy giving a low probability to going to Ann's party, Brian will respond by choosing not to go to the party, so that once again the likely outcome will be undesirable. What then is she to do? She needs a strategy that leaves Brian indifferent between choosing to go to the party and choosing not to go, that affords him the same expected value whatever he chooses. Similarly, Brian needs a strategy that leaves Jane indifferent between choosing to go to the party and choosing not to go. If Brian is indifferent as to his choice of strategy, then any strategy is a best response for him; similarly, if Jane is indifferent as to her choice of strategy, then any strategy is a best response for her. Therefore if each chooses a strategy that leaves the other indifferent, each strategy must be a best response to the other, so that the pair constitutes a Nash-equilibrium set.

Jane does not first form an expectation about Brian's choice of strategy and then choose her best response to it. Instead she chooses a strategy that leaves Brian nothing to choose among his responses. And Brian chooses a strategy that leaves Jane nothing to choose among her responses. In situations such as the one we are considering, it is always possible to find a strategy that leaves the other indifferent, and such strategies are mutual best responses, so that successful egoistic choice seems possible.

If we make not implausible assumptions about the relative values, to Jane and to Brian, of the possible outcomes of their choices, we might find that Jane should choose a mixed strategy with probability 2/7 of going to the party and 5/7 of not going, and that Brian should choose a mixed strategy with probability 3/5 of going to the party and 2/5 of not going.[17] And these strategies would constitute the unique Nash-equilibrium pair. If either were able to calculate one of these strategies, she or he would have sufficient knowledge of the situation to calculate the other. Neither Jane nor Brian need be concerned to conceal the choice of strategy from the other. Of course, at some point each must determine what actually to *do* — no doubt using a handy pocket randomizing device appropriately programmable for any lottery. We must suppose that the outcome of this determination remains unknown to the other until the action is actually carried out. In supposing that each chooses a strategy, we suppose that each considers the other's choice of a strategy, forming expectations about it but not any more determinate expectations. If Brian could know that Jane's handy randomizer said "Go!", then, rather than consulting his own, he would simply head for Ann's party.

We have no reason to assume that Jane and Brian actually have the information about each other's values needed to calculate strategies in Nash-equilibrium. And this is a very simple interaction. In more complex situations the procedure required to determine strategies in Nash-equilibrium may be more difficult,

---

[17] These mixed strategies yield equilibrium for the following case. Arbitrarily assigning the value 1 to an actor's most favoured outcome, and 0 to the least favoured outcome, we find that an interval measure of Jane's preferences assigns 1 to going to Ann's party if Brian does not, 1/2 to not going if Brian goes, 1/4 to not going if Brian does not, and 0 to going if Brian goes. And we find that an interval measure of Brian's preferences assigns 1 to going to Ann's party if Jane goes, 1/2 to not going if Jane does not, 1/10 to going if Jane does not, and 0 to not going if Jane does. Jane's mixed strategy affords Brian an expected utility of 5/14 whatever he does, and Brian's mixed strategy affords Jane an expected utility of 2/5 whatever she does. Note that the utility values for Jane and Brian are *not* interpersonally comparable; we may not infer that Jane may expect to do better from the situation than Brian from the fact that 2/5 is greater than 5/14.

even if the information needed is available. We know from Nash's proof that there must be at least one Nash-equilibrium strategy set, but this knowledge may have no practical application. Thus I make no claim about the ability of actual egoists to choose best response strategies. But there is a fundamental difference between recognizing that failure does occur and demonstrating that it *must* occur. There is a principle for choice among strategies that includes in its domain all of the sets of alternative strategies making up an interaction, and that takes, as values, sub-sets each of which has as members only strategies belonging also to Nash-equilibrium sets for the interaction. Egoists are no longer set a task that is insoluble in principle.

To avoid possible misunderstanding, note that the strategic consistency of egoism can in no way affect the impossibility, in some situations, of actually selecting only actions that meet the egoistic requirement. When Jane and Brian actually act, and discover what each other does, then one will not maximize value given the other's behaviour. Moving to the strategic level does not enlarge the actual possibilities for action, and so does not affect the impossibility of successful informed maximization by both Jane and Brian in terms of their actions. But if each selects a strategy that is a best response to the other's selection, then each will know that whatever the outcome, she or he maximized expected value. Neither will judge his or her choice to have failed *as a choice*.

Before we conclude this round of our argument, we should admit that we have not shown the existence of a principle for egoistic choice among strategies that includes all sets of alternative strategies in all interactions in its domain. All that we have shown is that the requirement that the strategies selected by the principle for any interaction form a Nash-equilibrium set can be satisfied. But we must not suppose that a sufficient principle of egoistic choice would simply require each actor to select a strategy — any strategy — belonging to such a set. For although this would suffice in the simple situation we have considered, in which there is but one Nash-equilibrium pair of strategies, yet in other more complex situations there may be a multitude of sets, each of which contains only strategies that are best responses to each other, but such that a strategy belonging to one Nash-equilibrium set is not a best response to strategies belonging to other Nash-equilibrium sets. Consider, for example, a situation in which several persons want to meet but are indifferent among several possible meeting-places. If each chooses to go to the same possible meeting-place, then each action is a best response to the others; if each chooses to go to a different meeting-place, then the actions are not best responses. We have not considered how egoists, embarrassed by such riches, would select among different sets of actions or strategies in Nash-equilibrium. Thus the present round of our argument concludes only with the judgement that the accusation of inconsistency against egoism is not proven. We have a Scots verdict.

7. An exhaustive examination of the problems created for egoists by the existence in some situations of several sets of actions or strategies, each in Nash-equilibrium, is beyond the scope of our present enquiry. I shall focus on but one such problem, arising from the plausible requirement that egoists coordinate their choices to bring about a mutually superior Nash-equilibrium, should one exist and should each stand to lose from the failure to coordinate.[18]

Let us begin by considering a simple game. Two players are each given a coin and must choose whether to show heads or to show tails. No communication between them is permitted; each must choose in ignorance of the other's choice. If both show the same, then each wins a sum of money, but the sum is larger if

---

[18] The problem discussed in this section is essentially the same as that discussed in my paper "The Impossibility of Rational Egoism," *Journal of Philosophy* 71 (1974), pp. 439–56. This earlier paper examines certain details not treated here, but focusses less clearly on the issue identified here as the consistent application of a principle for choice to an interaction and its sub-interactions.

both show heads. If one shows heads and the other shows tails, then each loses a sum of money. In this game there are two pairs of actions in Nash-equilibrium — each showing heads, and each showing tails. But the former pair is a superior equilibrium, dominating the latter, since the outcome if each shows heads has greater value for each player than the outcome if each shows tails. A principle of choice for egoists must surely accommodate this. We might initially suggest that such a principle must require the selection of strategies that will ensure coordination on a superior equilibrium, should there be one and should it satisfy certain accessibility considerations that we may ignore here.[19] Thus we suppose that in this game rational egoists choose heads.

A variant on our game may suggest that the proposed coordination requirement is too strong for egoists. Suppose that each player gains a sum of money if the other shows heads and loses an equivalent sum if the other shows tails. In this game every pair of strategies is in Nash-equilibrium, since each player is entirely indifferent about his own choice; what he gets is determined by what the other does. There is a unique equilibrium superior to all others, arising if each player shows heads. But the requirement that players coordinate on this equilibrium is egoistically unmotivated. Neither player has any incentive to show heads, since showing tails would neither reduce his expected value nor affect the occurrence of equilibrium. In this game we have no reason to suppose that rational egoists would choose heads rather than tails.

Intuitively, we want to treat coordination on strategies belonging to a set in superior Nash-equilibrium as an egoistic require-

---

[19] Consider a situation with three outcomes resulting from sets of strategies in Nash-equilibrium. Let the outcomes be P, Q, and R, and let P and Q be indifferent (from the standpoint of each individual) but superior to R. If communication is impossible, and if neither P nor Q possesses any naturally salient feature, then coordination may be possible only on the inferior equilibrium R, because its very inferiority distinguishes it, whereas nothing distinguishes P from Q. Here P and Q are effectively inaccessible; without communication neither can be singled out as a target for coordination.

ment only if defection from such coordination would reduce the defector's expected value. I shall not however attempt to formulate this requirement precisely, since it will be clear, in the situation we are about to consider and that poses a problem for the consistency of egoism, that coordination is egoistically motivated.

Consider now a more complex game, in which three players, A, B, and C, are each given a coin, and must choose, without communication, whether to show heads or to show tails. The values, or payoffs, of the possible outcomes of the different combinations of actions are shown in this table:

Action (= Pure strategy)			*Payoff*		
A	*B*	*C*	*A*	*B*	*C*
H	H	H	$1.00	$1.00	$1.00
H	H	T	$1.50	$1.50	0
H	T	H	−$1.50	−$1.50	0
T	H	H	−$1.50	−$1.50	0
H	T	T	$1.50	−$3.00	$1.00
T	H	T	−$3.00	$1.50	$1.00
T	T	H	$1.50	$1.50	0
T	T	T	$1.00	$1.00	$1.00

In this game there is a single set of strategies in Nash-equilibrium; each player shows heads. This is easily verified; showing heads is each player's best response if the others show heads, so the set is in equilibrium. It is unique since, given any other set, at least one player would do better to change her response, so the other set of strategies is not in Nash-equilibrium.

Let us suppose then that A expects C to show heads. For A reasons that if expectations are correct, and if each choice is a best response to the others, then the strategies must be in Nash-equilibrium, and showing heads yields the unique Nash-equilibrium. But then she notes that *if* C shows heads, then she and B would each do better were they to show tails. For then they would take C's winnings and add them to their own, gaining $1.50 instead of $1.00. Taking C's choice as fixed by the requirement of equilibrium, and focussing then solely on the interaction between A and B, the payoffs for the possible outcomes are shown in this table:

Action		*Payoff*	
A	*B*	*A*	*B*
H	H	$1.00	$1.00
H	T	−$1.50	−$1.50
T	H	−$1.50	−$1.50
T	T	$1.50	$1.50

In this sub-game there are two pairs of strategies in Nash-equilibrium — each player shows heads, and each shows tails. But the latter pair dominates the first; it is a superior equilibrium. And coordination on it is egoistically motivated; each stands to gain from achieving coordination and to lose if she defects from it. If A expects B's reasoning to parallel her own, then she concludes that, given that C may be expected to show heads, then she should show tails with the expectation that B also will show tails.

But C's deliberation need not have ceased with the realization that the requirement of equilibrium determines that she show heads. For if she correctly anticipates the reasoning of A and B, leading them to coordinate on tails, then she must conclude that she too should show tails. If she expects them to show tails, then showing tails is her best response, enabling her to keep a gain of $1.00 rather than losing it to A and B. But then if A and B anticipate this further deliberation by C, they should coordinate on heads; expecting C to show tails, they realize that their strategy pair showing heads now dominates the pair showing tails, since it enables them to recapture C's gain. And if C anticipates this further deliberation on the part of A and B, then, expecting them to show heads, she too should show heads. Thus she returns to the set of strategies in Nash-equilibrium, the point of departure for the circle that we have traced.

Crucial to the argument implicit in our discussion of this game is a claim about the consistency required for a principle of choice to be successfully employed. Suppose that a principle includes in its domain all of the sets of strategies constituting an interaction. Thus for each actor it yields a sub-set of his strategies as his choice set. Let each sub-set contain a single strategy; this will arise if the principle satisfies the Nash-equilibrium requirement and the situation has a unique Nash-equilibrium. Suppose that one actor chooses the unique strategy in his choice set, as the principle requires. Taking that choice as a fixed circumstance, apply the principle to the reduced interaction among the remaining actors. Then our claim is that, if the principle is consistent, it must yield, for each remaining actor, a choice set that contains the strategy in his original choice set. The principle must yield consistent guidance, whether an actor apply it directly to his choice of strategy in an overall interaction, or whether, taking for granted that some others will conform to it, he apply it to his choice of strategy in the resulting sub-interaction. A principle that says, "Everyone should show heads, but if actor C shows heads then everyone else should show tails," is inconsistent.

If we accept this view of consistency, then no egoistic principle of action can be both complete and consistent. An egoistic principle must satisfy the equilibrium requirement, that strategies chosen in an interaction be mutual best responses, and the coordination requirement, that strategies chosen yield a superior equilibrium, if one exists and defection from it would be costly to the defector. A complete principle of choice for interaction must yield a non-empty choice set for each set of strategies in each possible interaction. A consistent principle of choice must yield compatible choice sets when applied to an interaction as a whole and to any reduced sub-interaction resulting from taking its application to some of those interacting as given. Our game of matching coins shows that egoism, completeness, and consistency are jointly incompatible.

Egoists seek individually advantageous responses to the actions of their fellows and mutually beneficial coordination among their actions. These goals prove to be in conflict in situations such as the game we have discussed. Of course, the failure to attain a goal can be accepted. But we have shown that in some situations, some actors can not do as well for themselves as possible, given what the others do. If A, B, and C do not all show heads, then at least one could do better given the possibilities left open by the others' choices. If A, B, and C do all show heads, then A and B could coordinate on a mutually better outcome. In such a situation, egoism makes inconsistent demands, and so fails.

8. So what can an egoist do? Why, he can do his best. But we now know that this answer misleads. We have discovered situations in which not everyone *can* do his best. *Any* person can do his best, but *not every* person can. If we ask, what can *egoists* do, we must not reply that *they* can do their best.

Let us change the question. What can egoists choose? If we take strategies as the objects of choice, then we can answer: they can choose their best. But again we know that the answer misleads. We have discovered situations in which everyone can choose her best, given all other choices, but only if some fail to coordinate their choices on what is, for them, mutually best. And were they to succeed in coordinating, then some individual would fail to choose her best. Taken individually egoists can choose their best; taken, let us say, coordinatively, not all egoists can.

Faced with the complexities of strategic interaction, the egoist must soon lose the naïve hope of formulating a complete and consistent principle for choice satisfying the conditions implicit in his egoistic stance. The problem proves less tractable than either philosophical critics or proponents of egoism have recognized. Perhaps, then, the first lesson for the would-be egoist is to place less trust in the words of philosophers and pay closer attention to the structures of interaction exhibited by game theorists. But the message our game-theoretic enquiry conveys must surely dishearten him: anyone may do his best, but not everyone.

Yet may not his dismay and puzzlement remain only that? The demonstrably impossible is, simply, impossible. The egoist can do his best. That the structures of interaction constrain doing one's best in initially unexpected ways neither contracts nor expands the real horizons that egoists, in their actions and choices, have always faced.

This would dismiss too easily the import of our argument. Egoists, and not egoists alone but all would-be maximizers of actor-relative value, have been on the whole unaware of the structure of their predicament. They have recognized problems arising from the incompatibility of their professed values; some have interpreted this incompatibility as a sign of irrationality, some have seen it only as the basis of inevitable frustration. They have not, however, recognized the constraints that exist on doing, and choosing, one's best. They have not recognized that the very correctness of the expectations persons may form about the choices of those with whom they interact may ensure that someone must fail to *do* what would maximize his value, given the possibilities left open to him by those expected choices. They have not recognized that a full awareness of the possibilities for advantageous coordination may ensure that either someone fails to choose what would maximize his value given the choices of others, or that some fail to choose what would be mutually maximizing given the choices of others.

A principle that prescribes a choice for each and then, on the assumption that some follow it, prescribes a different choice for the others, forces more than dismay and puzzlement on those who would adhere to it. The inconsistency of egoistic principles requires us to think again about certain failures of interaction, to reappraise what goes wrong in the light of the inescapable nature of certain conflicts. Even if anyone can do his best, the fact that not everyone can do his best forces us to reconsider the attribution of responsibility for failure in situations comparable to those we have examined. We excuse, or partially excuse, a person's failure to achieve his objective, if we find that he did his best; must we now excuse a person's failure to do his best, if we find that not everyone could?

Here I leave these and other implications of our discussion of the inconsistency of egoism to the reader's reflection. Perhaps, just as we found a partial remedy for the failure of egoistic choice among actions by considering choice among strategies, so we might be able to find a partial remedy for the conflict between individual maximization and mutual coordination. We must not draw too firm a conclusion to our treatment of the consistency of egoism, and so we must hesitate in assessing its implications for such issues as the attribution of responsibility. But we put these issues aside in part because an even more pressing question awaits us. If there are limits to what egoists can do and can choose, yet in many situations all can indeed do their best. But should they? The would-be egoist who as yet sees no reason to change his ways may yet have to reconsider if those ways can be shown to be self-defeating.

II. WHAT SHOULD AN EGOIST DO?

1. "The very *raison d'être* of a morality is to yield reasons which overrule the reasons of self-interest in those cases when everyone's following self-interest would be harmful to everyone." [20] As a claim about actual moralities, this statement by Kurt

---

[20] Kurt Baier, *The Moral Point of View: A Rational Basis of Ethics* (Ithaca, N.Y.: Cornell University Press, 1958), p. 309.

Baier may well be false, or at most a very partial truth. But as a claim about rational morality — about a morality that would be acceptable to rational actors — this statement is, I believe, the exact truth. A rational morality is a constraint, or set of constraints, on the maximization of actor-relative value with which it is rational for would-be maximizers of such value to agree and comply.

But how can it be rational for maximizers to constrain their maximizing activity — or, more specifically in terms of our enquiry, for egoists to constrain their egoism? I propose to answer this question. But for some years I thought no answer was possible. Indeed, I said as much.

When I first considered Kurt Baier's conception of morality, I found myself trying to understand the conflict between reasons of self-interest and overriding reasons, and I wrote, and read, a paper in which the issues became obscured in a labyrinth of words. After listening to those words, Howard Sobel took me aside and, quickly sketching a matrix on a sheet of paper, said, "Look! You're talking about the Prisoners' Dilemma." And I looked, and it was as if scales fell from my eyes and I received sight.[21]

But at first I saw poorly. I saw in the Prisoners' Dilemma a clear representation of the conflict between interested reasons and moral or cooperative reasons, but neither seemed overriding. I saw a conflict between two conceptions of rationality — the one individual and prudential, the other collective and moral. And I said that "the individual who needs a reason for being moral which is not itself a moral reason cannot have it. . . . For it is more than apparently paradoxical to suppose that considerations of advantage could ever of themselves justify accepting a real disadvantage."[22] I was wrong. It is that supposedly genuine

---

[21] The incident described here occurred at the University of California, Los Angeles, probably in November 1965.

[22] David Gauthier, "Morality and Advantage," *Philosophical Review* vol. 76 (1967), p. 470.

paradox that I want now to confute — to show that one can and does have a non-moral reason for being moral, a reason that must be recognized even by the egoist.

Egoism is self-defeating. The objective of the egoist is to do as well for himself as possible, to maximize actor-relative value. More typically we think of the egoist as identifying his interest or his advantage with what he values, so that his objective is simply to maximize that interest or advantage. But the egoist falls short of this objective — and falls farther short than some who are not egoists. Reflecting on his maximizing objective, the egoist finds reason to change his ways, casting off the egoistic scales from his eyes and seeing as a moral being — even as a being who accepts real disadvantages. The egoist, embarked on the journey of rational choice, finds, contrary to all expectation, that his destination is moral theory.

To show that egoism is self-defeating is no simple matter. As we shall see, it is not enough to show that egoists, in maximizing actor-relative value, fail to do as well for themselves *collectively* as they might. It is not enough to show, in Baier's words, that "everyone's following self-interest would be harmful to everyone." We must rather show that each person's following self-interest is harmful to himself, that each fails to do as well for himself *individually* as he might. Only an argument addressed to the individual egoist can hope to show that *his* ways are self-defeating. But we may begin from the perspective of everyone, from the failure of egoists to do as well for themselves as possible, and then show how this perspective may be linked to that of the individual. And so we may begin with the Prisoners' Dilemma.

2. If philosophers have paid little attention to considerations of Nash-equilibrium in examining the consistency of egoism, they have become quite familiar with the Prisoners' Dilemma as exhibiting the seemingly self-defeating character of egoistic behaviour. Let us review exactly what the Dilemma shows. Each prisoner — Jack and Zack as I called them in the preceding

part — has a strategy that is a best response to whatever strategy the other chooses. This strategy is confession. But the outcome if each chooses his best response is disadvantageous to both. Both would do better if both chose the alternative strategy — non-confession or silence. Each does best to confess whatever the other does, but each does better if neither confesses than if both confess.

We need another piece of terminology to talk about the Dilemma — Pareto-optimality.[23] An outcome is Pareto-optimal if and only if no feasible alternative affords some person greater value and no person lesser value. Or, assuming a link between value and preference, if and only if no alternative would be preferred by some and dispreferred by none. An equivalent formulation is that an outcome is Pareto-optimal if and only if every feasible alternative that affords some person greater value also affords some other person lesser value.

Consider the outcomes possible for Jack and Zack. If both confess, each receives a heavy sentence, but short of the maximum. If neither confesses, each receives a light sentence, but exceeding the minimum. If one confesses and the other does not, the one confessing receives the minimum sentence and the other receives the maximum. Let us assume that their values are related inversely to the length of their sentences. Then if we consider in turn each pair of outcomes, we find that in every case Jack prefers one member of the pair and Zack the other, except that both prefer the outcome if neither confesses to the outcome if both confess. The outcome of mutual confession is therefore *not* Pareto-optimal; there is an alternative affording both greater value. Every other outcome *is* Pareto-optimal; for each such outcome, every alternative affording one prisoner greater value affords the other lesser value.

---

[23] The term "Pareto-optimality" refers to Vilfredo Pareto, who did not talk about optimality at all, but rather ophelimity.

But the strategies leading to confession are in Nash-equilibrium; each is the best response to the other. And since each is the unique best response whatever the other prisoner chooses, no other set of strategies is in Nash-equilibrium. The outcomes thus divide into two exclusive and exhaustive sets — the set of Pareto-optimal outcomes and the set of outcomes resulting from strategies in Nash-equilibrium. That the sets are exhaustive is not a common characteristic of structures of interaction. But that the sets are exclusive is common, or at least not uncommon, and represents that feature of the Prisoners' Dilemma that makes it a supposed dilemma. For if, as I have argued, informed egoists are restricted to outcomes resulting from strategies in Nash-equilibrium, then in such situations as the Dilemma, egoists are barred from Pareto-optimality. Each may succeed in doing as well for himself as he can, but everyone could do better.

An outcome may be conceived in two quite different ways, each important to rationality. On the one hand, an outcome may be conceived as the product of the members of a set of strategies; on the other hand, it may be conceived as a set of payoffs. Conceived as the product of a set of strategies, we say that it is in Nash-equilibrium if and only if each strategy maximizes the actor's value given the other strategies. Considered as a set of payoffs, we say that it is Pareto-optimal if and only if each payoff maximizes the recipient's value given the other payoffs.[24] No complete principle for choice in interaction takes every set of alternative strategies into a (non-empty) choice set, some member of which belongs also to a Nash-equilibrium set that yields a Pareto-optimal outcome. No complete principle can ensure both Nash-equilibrium and Pareto-optimality in every interaction. This is the impossibility theorem, illustrated by the Prisoners' Dilemma, that egoists and all maximizers of actor-relative value must face.

---

[24] This is true only if payoff functions are continuous. More generally, an outcome is Pareto-optimal if and only if each payoff maximizes the recipient's value on condition that no other payoff is decreased.

Note that this impossibility does not reveal a further inconsistency in egoism. The problem here is not similar to those discussed in the preceding part. There is no difficulty in formulating an egoistic principle for choice in the Prisoner's Dilemma and similar situations of incompatibility between equilibrium and optimality. The equilibrium requirement for an egoistic principle is straightforwardly satisfied, with no need to resort to strategies rather than to actions as the objects of choice. And the equilibrium requirement suffices to determine an egoistic principle; coordination is irrelevant in the Dilemma. The coordination requirement for egoistic principles of choice that I introduced in the preceding part applies to certain situations with more than one Nash-equilibrium strategy set. But in the Dilemma there is only one equilibrium set. Egoists, as maximizers of actor-relative value, are able to coordinate their strategies only within the limits allowed by the requirement that each actor consider his strategy to be a best response to the strategies he expects the others to choose. If, as in the Dilemma, each actor has a unique best response whatever he expects the others to choose, then coordination has no place.

Let us illustrate the difference between a simple coordination problem and the Dilemma by contrasting two games. First, consider again the two-person game of matching coins that served in Part I, section 7, to motivate the coordination requirement, here with determinate monetary values.

Action		Payoff	
A	B	A	B
H	H	$2	$2
H	T	−$2	−$2
T	H	−$2	−$2
T	T	$1	$1

Here each does best to show what the other shows; this assures equilibrium. Both do better if both show heads than if both show tails; mutually beneficial coordination thus enables the players to select among the equilibrium strategy sets. But now consider this Dilemma-type game:

Action		Payoff	
A	B	A	B
H	H	$2	$2
H	T	-$3	$3
T	H	$3	-$3
T	T	$1	$1

Here again both do better if both show heads than if both show tails. But this consideration never enters into an egoistic principle for choice. For each does best to show tails whatever the other does; this alone assures equilibrium. And so the equilibrium requirement leaves no room for other considerations. Egoists should *not* show heads, because showing heads does not lead either player to do as well for himself as he can. The outcome of egoistic behaviour may well be regarded by the players as unfortunate, but in choosing tails, each does his best for himself. But should he? Should he *be* an egoist?   ꝛꝛ5/08

Before attempting to answer this question, we must generalize from the particular structure of the Dilemma to the underlying conflict between Nash-equilibrium and Pareto-optimality that it illustrates. And we must not misunderstand the nature of this conflict. An egoist concerned to maximize actor-relative value is utterly indifferent to both equilibrium and optimality. He cares only for his own payoff. If the strategies of others are given, then he chooses that strategy most profitable to himself; if all behave in this way, then Nash-equilibrium is the unintended result. If the payoffs of others were given and he were to choose among payoffs, then he would choose that most profitable to himself; if all behaved in this way, then Pareto-optimality would be the unintended result. The egoist is concerned with payoffs, but since choice determines actions or strategies, he can express his concern with payoffs only in his choice among strategies. What the Dilemma reveals is that in some situations, his choice does not give effective expression to his concern. Selecting among strategies, the egoist may be unable to maximize his payoff given the payoffs of others, and so may be unable to obtain some benefit that he could enjoy at no cost to others. Let us then say that the egoist faces *strategy–payoff conflict*. This is the general problem that the Dilemma reveals.

3. How important is strategy–payoff conflict? Grant that its occurrence must complicate life for egoists and indeed for all maximizers of actor-relative value. But does it occur, except in the structures of interaction studied by game theorists? If it is a phenomenon of no practical significance, then it can hardly serve as the basis for an argument that egoism is self-defeating.

It does occur. Indeed, strategy–payoff conflict is a fundamental phenomenon of social life. It constitutes the core of the problem of ensuring the optimal supply of public or collective goods. It explains the sub-optimality that characteristically results from failures to internalize effects — the coincidence of net social costs from pollution with net individual benefits to polluters. It is at the heart of Garrett Hardin's tragedy of the commons,[25] and helps explain John Kenneth Galbraith's observation that an affluent society enjoys "private opulence and public squalor." [26] It enables us to understand why even a government that spent its funds wisely would need an I.R.S. to collect them. Free-riders and parasites flourish in the context of strategy–payoff conflict.

[25] See "The Tragedy of the Commons," *Science* 162 (1968), pp. 1243–48.
[26] See *The Affluent Society* (Boston: Houghton Mifflin, 1958), p. 257. Galbraith does not, however, focus on this explanation.

Its importance, widely recognized today, was long obscured in much of our social and economic thought. There are two principal reasons for this. First, economists since Adam Smith have tended to focus unduly on the perfectly competitive market — from which strategy–payoff conflict is blissfully absent. As Russell Hardin has dramatically expressed it, the Prisoners' Dilemma is the back of the Invisible Hand.[27] In the perfect market the Invisible Hand ensures that if each pursues his own interest, the social interest is furthered, albeit unintentionally. We may make this more precise by saying that market activity — in which each individual seeks to maximize the value of a function defined over the goods he consumes and the factor services he provides — leads to an outcome on society's utility-possibility frontier, so that no person's position could be improved without worsening that of some other person. The equilibrium resulting after all voluntary exchanges is Pareto-optimal.

Were the world to be, as some economists of the Chicago school are alleged to suppose that it is, a perfectly competitive market, then egoists would have no reason to change their straightforwardly maximizing ways. The Prisoners' Dilemma would be a logical curiosity, revealing the possibility of interactions, happily never realized, in which egoists would fail to end up on the utility-possibility frontier and so would fail, collectively, to do as well for themselves as possible. But illuminating as the market is in showing us the possibility of interactions that give rise to no problems for maximizers of actor-relative value — indeed, illuminating as the market is in revealing to us a type of interaction that would not need to be guided by those principles, constraining maximizing behaviour, that constitute a rational morality — yet to most of us the real world does not seem to be a very close approximation to the realm of perfect competition. And so we expect to face strategy–payoff conflicts,

---

[27] See *Collective Action* (Baltimore: Johns Hopkins University Press, 1982), page 7.

both in our everyday interactions and in the design of the social institutions that frame those interactions.

But even when we turn away from the perfect market, we encounter a second factor that has obscured our awareness of this conflict. For awareness of the failure of the market as a model for much of our social interaction does not entail awareness of the core problem facing non-market public or collective behaviour. There is a strong temptation to suppose that, just as a rational individual will, within the limits of available information, so choose that he does as well for himself as possible, so a group of rational individuals will also choose that they do as well for themselves as possible. We extrapolate from individual action to group or collective action.

Mancur Olson, Jr., in his book *The Logic of Collective Action*, written some twenty years ago, seems to have been the first to recognize the general fallacy involved in this extrapolation.[28] Here I shall illustrate it with an example adapted, not from his work, but from that of Russell Hardin.[29] Suppose that 10 units of a pure public good in full joint supply are available to a community of 10 persons. Each unit costs $5 and affords each member of the community a benefit of $1. Each must decide whether to contribute $5 to the social provision of the good. If all contribute, total benefit is $100 and cost $50, for a net social benefit of $50 and a net benefit to each individual of $5. If no one contributes, then net social and individual benefit are both $0. Nevertheless, no one who seeks to maximize his payoff will contribute. Each reasons that n other persons will contribute, where n takes a value from 0 to 9. If he also contributes, net social benefit is $10(n+1)$, divided so that net benefit to each contributing individual is $(n-4)$ and to each non-contributor $(n+1)$. If he does not contribute, net social benefit is $10n$ divided so that net

<hr />

[28] *The Logic of Collective Action* (Cambridge: Harvard University Press, 1965); the fallacy is spelled out in the Introduction, pp. 1–2.

[29] *Collective Action*, pp. 25–27.

benefit to each contributing individual is $\$(n-5)$ and to each non-contributor $\$n$. Thus, if he contributes, his net benefit is $\$(n-4)$; if he does not contribute, his net benefit is $\$n$. For all possible values of n, $\$n$ is greater than $\$(n-4)$, so he chooses not to contribute.

The parallel with reasoning in the Prisoners' Dilemma should be evident. Given a pure public good, each individual chooses to ride free; of course the result is that there is nothing on which to ride. I have considered only an artificially simple case; in more realistic cases in which the value of each unit of the good diminishes as more units are obtained, it may be that some units will be bought by individuals who find it worth their while to pay the entire cost of supplying the unit to everyone, but before optimal supply is reached, each will prefer to ride free at the current level of supply rather than to contribute an additional unit.

Recognition of the problem of collective action should dispel any temptation to suppose that my argument is addressed not to us, but only to very different persons — to egoists. We are, all of us, maximizers of actor-relative value — or a near approximation thereto — in many of our interactions. And we all face the problem of collective action posed by the back of the Invisible Hand. When we do, our behaviour tends to be, as the egoist's must be, self-defeating. Or so I claim. I must now make the claim good.

4. That egoism is self-defeating in situations involving strategy–payoff conflict may seem evident. For the outcome of egoistic interaction affords each actor a payoff less than he might obtain without the payoff of any other actor being in any way diminished. Everyone could gain; net benefits are possible but not provided. Each, then, does not do as well for himself as possible, and so egoistic behaviour defeats its own end. The egoist aims at maximizing his value and achieves less than the non-egoist who aims instead at Pareto-optimality.

We should not be convinced by this argument. *Each* does not *get* as much as possible, and *all* do not *do* as well for themselves as possible; it does not follow that *each* fails to *do* as well for himself as possible. To show that egoism is self-defeating we must consider, not its overall result, but the situation of the individual who must choose his response to the choices he expects his fellows to make. To consider the plight of egoists solely from the overall or collective standpoint is to commit a version of the fallacy exposed by Olson in his analysis of collective action. Naïvely, we supposed that a group of individuals maximize their overall net benefit in the same way that a single individual does. Realizing this to be fallacious, we may then suppose that an individual will fail to maximize net benefit in the same way that a group does. But just as what is maximizing from the standpoint of an individual need not be so from the standpoint of a group, so what is self-defeating from the standpoint of a group need not be so from the standpoint of an individual member. And only from this latter standpoint can we show an egoist that his way of acting is self-defeating.

The egoist tells us that we have shown nothing of the kind. He chooses his best response given his expectations of what the others will do. What more can he do for himself? The problem, if indeed it is a problem and not a simple misfortune, is that the choices of others lead to his getting less than he might, given their payoffs. He is the victim of their choices, not his own. They do not seek to victimize him; each in turn simply chooses as best he can for himself. Each is the victim of choices that do not take his benefits and costs into account. But to be victimized is not to engage in self-defeating behaviour. Indeed, were the egoist to complain to his fellows that they did not consider his costs and benefits, they would rightly reply that, were they to take more than their own interests into account, then they would truly be engaged in self-defeating behaviour.

Egoists are defeated by the existence of strategy–payoff conflict. But no individual egoist is defeated. No individual can improve his own lot. The remedy is not for individuals to choose differently, in a non-egoistic way, but rather for them to prevent strategy–payoff conflicts from arising. Those who would otherwise expect to find themselves paying the costs of such conflicts may have good reason to provide for sanctions, through binding agreements or external enforcement, that alter the payoffs so that strategies in Nash-equilibrium lead to a Pareto-optimal outcome. These are the classic devices, proposed by Thomas Hobbes long before the theory of games revealed the precise structure giving rise to conflict. Covenants — but not covenants without the sword, for they are but words of no strength to secure a man — and the sovereign who enforces covenants and structures social institutions to prevent free-riding bring order to the egoists' world.[30] These precautionary devices themselves involve costs that egoists would prefer to avoid, and Hobbes may be accused of failing to give sufficient consideration to these costs,[31] but the world is under no obligation to accommodate itself to all of our preferences. There is nothing self-defeating in the need to cope with structures of interaction that in themselves impede persons seeking the greatest possible realization of their actor-relative values.

The charge that egoism is self-defeating seems to rest on confusion. We must distinguish between the choices of individuals and the structures within which they choose. The claim that egoism is self-defeating is a claim about the effects of egoistic choices. It can not be supported merely by pointing to the effects of strategy–payoff conflict. These effects determine the possibilities for choice; within these the egoist does the best he can. He would do better were the possibilities otherwise, were the world a perfect market.

The sensible egoist may of course seek to convince his fellows that egoism is a self-defeating policy. Aware of the costs they inflict on him, he may in his own interest seek to persuade them

---

[30] See Thomas Hobbes, *Leviathan* (London: 1651), chs. 15, 17.

[31] But Hobbes does give some consideration to this matter. At the end of *Leviathan*, ch. 18, he notes that "the estate of Man can never be without some incommodity or other," and goes on to compare the costs of government with those of civil war and the absence of all authority.

not to impose such costs. He may appeal to the idea of strategy–payoff conflict in the hope of convincing them that, since everyone ends up worse off than need be, their egoism is self-defeating. But his appeal is purely specious, intended to secure for himself the benefits of non-egoistic behaviour by others, while continuing clear-headedly to displace what costs he can upon them — save that he must appear to practice what he preaches to enhance the effectiveness of his preaching. The claim that egoism is self-defeating is, it may now seem, not merely a misunderstanding of the nature of strategy–payoff conflict, but the egoist's deliberate distortion of its real character.

5. The egoist's defence is mistaken. He does not do as well for himself as he could. The reader will no doubt be on his guard when I claim this; perhaps I am the egoist seeking to sucker him or her with my honeyed words. Against this suspicion I can but offer argument. And the key to my argument is this. An egoist will of course maximize actor-relative value whenever he can. Putting to one side those situations in which egoism may fail to offer consistent guidance to choice, let us agree that in each situation the egoist chooses a best response to the choices he expects others to make, and that *in those situations* he can do no better. But his very way of choosing affects the situations in which he may expect to find himself. And the effects are to his disadvantage. The egoist makes the most of his opportunities, but as an egoist he finds those opportunities inferior to those of a non-egoist — not, to be sure, just any non-egoist, but one whom I shall call the cooperator. In making this clear we show the self-defeating character of egoism.

In the Prisoners' Dilemma we may distinguish a cooperative and a non-cooperative strategy for each actor. In the tale of Jack and Zack, the non-cooperative strategy is of course to confess; the cooperative strategy is to remain silent. We may be thankful if prisoners prove to be non-cooperators, if there is no honour among thieves, but in general, and always from the standpoints of those concerned, non-cooperation is costly. Two cooperators will each do better than two non-cooperators. The problem, as we have seen, is that a non-cooperator paired with a cooperator will do better still, and at the cooperator's expense.

Suppose then that an actor is *conditionally* disposed to cooperate in Prisoners' Dilemma situations, and more generally in all situations involving strategy–payoff conflict. She does not unthinkingly opt for a cooperative strategy. Instead, she forms an expectation about the strategy choices of her partners (or opponents) and conforms her own choice to that expectation. She chooses cooperation as a response to expected cooperation, and non-cooperation as a response to expected non-cooperation.

How does her conditionally cooperative disposition affect her payoffs? At first glance it may seem that it must reduce them. If she expects the other to choose a non-cooperative strategy, then she maximizes her expected payoff by her own choice. But if she expects the other actor to cooperate, then she does not maximize her expected payoff and so gains less than were she consistently to choose non-cooperation.

But this argument fails to take into account the disposition of the other actor or actors. Suppose that the other actor is also conditionally disposed to cooperation. Then were she disposed not to cooperate, and could expect him correctly to read her intention, she would expect him also not to cooperate, and so would expect to end up at the mutually disadvantageous outcome of strategies in Nash-equilibrium. But if she is disposed to cooperate, and again expects the other correctly to read her intention, then she expects him to cooperate and so she expects to end up at a mutually advantageous Pareto-optimal outcome. Among conditional cooperators, expectations about others' choices and dispositions to choose oneself are so related that each may benefit from interaction in ways that non-cooperators can not parallel.

The egoist seeks to maximize actor-relative value given his expectations about the strategies others will choose. But their choices, and so his expectations, may be affected by his egoistic, maximizing policy; others, anticipating his choice, respond in a maximizing manner. The cooperator refrains from seeking to maximize value given her expectations about the strategies others will choose. And their choices, and so her expectations, may be affected by her cooperative policy; other cooperators, anticipating her choice, respond in a cooperative manner. And so egoism is self-defeating. Our argument rests on a comparison between the effects of choosing on a maximizing, non-cooperative basis, and the effects of choosing on a conditionally cooperative basis. Although the conditional cooperator refrains from making the most of her opportunities, yet she finds herself with opportunities that the egoist lacks, and so may expect payoffs superior to those that he can attain.

Of course the conditional cooperator may err. She may fail to recognize the willingness of others to cooperate with her, and so treat them as egoists. She may fail to recognize the egoism of others, and, treating them as cooperators, be taken advantage of by them. Unless cooperators are reasonably capable of both identifying one another and singling out non-cooperators, their conditional disposition may prove disadvantageous. This is an empirical matter. However, given the real benefits of cooperation, we should expect would-be conditional cooperators to seek to improve their abilities both to identify the dispositions of those with whom they interact and to make their own disposition known. Although the actual advantageousness of conditional cooperation depends both on these abilities and on the proportion of cooperators in the interacting population, yet the potential advantageousness of the disposition is not empirically based, but reflects the logical structure of interaction. Ideally, an individual whose objective is egoistic, to do as well for himself as possible, must expect to do better, not as an egoist, but as a cooperator.

I claim, then, that given the capacity to choose between egoism and conditional cooperation, and given also sufficient ability to identify the dispositions of others and to make oneself identifiable in turn, a rational person will choose to dispose herself to conditional cooperation. This choice is itself an egoistic one; she maximizes her expected actor-relative value in so choosing among possible dispositions to choose. But its effect is to convert her from an egoist to a cooperator, to a person who, in appropriate circumstances, does not choose egoistically.

Before considering objections to this argument, I should note that it does *not* depend on the supposition that one may expect to find oneself in an indefinite sequence of strategy–payoff conflicts, so that by choosing to cooperate in a particular situation one affects the expectations, and so the choices, of others in subsequent situations. There has been considerable discussion of the importance of reputation in iterated or repeated Prisoners' Dilemmas and in situations in which one benefits from a credible deterrent threat — for example the market-entry situation discussed in Reinhard Selten's "Chain-store Paradox." [32] But our concern is not with reputation or threat. The rationale for choosing conditional cooperation over egoism does not depend on the supposition that one can gain long-term benefit by acquiring a reputation for making cooperative choices. My argument may be applied to a one-shot conflict. [33]

Suppose that each person were to know — we need not mind how — that once and only once in her life would she face a strategy–payoff conflict. If she could reliably identify the disposition of the other actors in that situation and could expect them to identify hers, then she would have reason to dispose herself to conditional cooperation. For were she able to do so, then, if her partners in the situation were also conditional cooperators, she would do better than were she a non-cooperator. And were her partners non-cooperators, then, since she would so identify them, she would do no worse than had she remained an egoist. Note

---

[32] See "The Chain-store Paradox," *Theory and Decision* 9 (1978), pp. 127–59.

[33] For the application to deterrence, see my paper "Deterrence, Maximization, and Rationality," to appear in *Ethics* 94 (1984), and in Douglas MacLean (ed.), *The Security Gamble: Deterrence in the Nuclear Age* (Totowa, N.J.: Rowman and Allanheld, in press).

that in this situation, if she finds herself among cooperators, she clearly does *not* maximize actor-relative value, whether in terms of her short-run expectations in the particular situation, or in terms of her long-run expectations for the remainder of her life. If she is genuinely disposed to cooperate, then in appropriate circumstances she does not behave in any way as an egoist.

Let us now turn to objections. It will no doubt be said that, although it may be rational to pretend to be a cooperator, yet it is not rational actually to be one. The rational egoist will not give up his egoism however much he may appear to do so. Now I do not deny that there can be circumstances in which pretence would be the rational policy for a maximizer of actor-relative value. But no argument has been, or can be, given to show that this must always be the case. Perhaps pretence will not work — the detecting capacities of others are too good. Or perhaps the psychological strain of pretence is simply too great. The best way to reap the advantages of cooperation may be to be a genuine cooperator. The honesty that is the best policy may prove to be the honesty that, once adopted, can not be cast aside.

It may then be said that our argument shows that the egoist must recognize the benefits, in appropriate circumstances, of disposing himself to conditional cooperation. But then egoism is not self-defeating. Rather it contains the resources for its own reform. The truest egoism is conditional cooperation. This objection interprets egoism very differently than I have done. In considering whether egoism is self-defeating, as in considering whether it is inconsistent, I have focussed on an egoistic principle for choice among strategies or actions. I have shown that it is self-defeating to be unconditionally disposed to act on such a principle — that is, on a principle satisfying the condition that it take each set of alternative possible strategies for an actor into a sub-set, the members of which maximize some actor-relative measure defined over the original set. I take egoism to be the unconditional disposition to act on such a principle. The person who, for whatever reason, chooses not to act on such a principle, chooses not to be an egoist. Her reason for so choosing may itself be egoistic, as may her choice not to be an egoist. But it is what she chooses, and not why or how she chooses it, that is decisive here; she is not an egoist if she does not choose an egoistic principle for choice.

Egoism does indeed contain the resources for its own reform. The egoist is able to recognize the self-defeating character of his disposition to choose, and so has reason to select an alternative disposition. But the reform that the egoist carries out is not one internal to his original egoistic position. Choosing conditional cooperation is the egoist's last act as an egoist, and in that act the self-defeating character of egoism is affirmed.

6. By limiting the pretension of egoism we enhance the prospect for morality. Were egoistic principles of choice not self-defeating, the moralist would find herself compelled to reject either an actor-relative conception of value or a maximizing conception of rationality. Morality, as I understand it here, provides an *internal* constraint on the straightforward attempt to do as well for oneself as possible. An internal constraint is one that falls between the actor's evaluation and her choice — a constraint, then, on her principle for choice, the function taking her sets of alternative strategies into choice sets. Such a constraint has no claim to the egoist's consideration. He does not consider the imposition of an *external* constraint unjustified, since for him all justification is actor-relative and those imposing the constraint may well find that it promotes their ends. But an external constraint affects either one's range of options, and so the strategies among which one can choose, or the value one may expect from the outcome of some of one's options. An external constraint thus leaves the egoist free to choose on the basis of his maximizing principle, and so leaves his egoism intact. But voluntary adherence to a constraint on maximization — a constraint leaving one's range of options and their values unaffected — is incompatible with egoism. If morality provides such an internal constraint, then a

moral principle for choice must be incompatible with, and so an
alternative to, an egoistic principle.

To avoid possible misunderstanding, let me note that in treating morality as an internal constraint on straightforward maximization, I am offering a necessary, but not a sufficient, characterization. Not every conceivable internal constraint would be
moral. I can not here offer a full account of what must be added
to the idea of an internal constraint to capture the concept of
morality; what I shall add will relate morality to cooperation.

In rejecting egoism the moralist has traditionally employed
one or both of two lines of attack. The first turns on the egoist's
conception of actor-relative value. As I noted in the first part,
some, such as G. E. Moore, profess to find this conception self-
contradictory, insisting that value must be absolute. Thus they
accuse the egoist of maximizing the fulfilment of his interest
rather than maximizing what is truly good. His interest may be
part of this good, but no more part than the interest of anyone
else. Others argue that the egoist mistakes his apparent interest
for his true interest and claim that each person's true interest is
linked to a transcendent, non-relative value in such a way that the
conflict between the apparent interests of individuals is replaced
by the harmonization of their true interests. This I believe to be
the position Plato advances in the *Republic*; thinkers of this persuasion accuse the egoist of maximizing the fulfilment of apparent
good rather than true good.

The second line of attack turns on the egoist's conception of
maximizing rationality. Some, such as Kant, would argue that the
egoist mistakenly supposes reason to be merely instrumental,
determining the means appropriate to given ends, so that he fails
to recognize that reason has a practical role quite independent of
that set it by interest.[34] Morality, on this view, arises from the

[34] This paragraph is intended as an interpretation of Kant's position as he
develops it in the *Groundwork of the Metaphysic of Morals* and the *Critique of
Practical Reason*, but it is not my concern here to offer any defence of whatever con-

ascription to practical rationality of the same universality found in theoretical rationality. As theoretical reason discovers descriptive or explanatory laws, so practical reason discovers prescriptive or justificatory laws. The egoist's commitment to maximization is thus rejected as insufficient for the universality inherent in true rationality.

Neither of these lines of attack on egoism seems promising to me. Fortunately, I need not argue that claim here; it would be absurd and presumptuous to think that I could dispose of two of the main traditions of moral thought in a few words. Instead I can bypass them. Allowing the egoist his conception of actor-relative value and of maximizing rationality, I have shown that if he does not give up his egoism in favour of conditional cooperation, then he bars himself from opportunities for advantageous interaction with his fellows. Adherence to a principle for choice that places appropriate constraints on maximizing behaviour may be expected to benefit the adherent. And so I find a place for internal constraint, for a non-maximizing moral principle for choice, by arguing from the egoist's premisses to the rejection of his conclusions.

I can then suggest that my attack on the egoist requires assumptions far weaker than those necessary to the attacks mounted by traditional moralists. Where they assault his position from without, seeking to batter down his premisses, I undermine it from within, showing that the premisses give it no support. I need neither absolute value nor universalized rationality. I can then suggest that moral theorists have resorted to these lines of attack because they have not seen the possibility of defending morality by fighting the egoist on his own ground. And so I can suggest that the appeal of both the Platonic and the Kantian traditions

---

troversial features the interpretation contains. Whether or not the account is faithful to Kant, it seems to me to raise important questions about the instrumentality of practical reason, and the connection of practical and theoretical reason, that deserve non-Kantian answers.

has depended on the failure to recognize a third way by which the moralist may snatch value and reason from the egoist's grasp.

To add substance to these suggestions, let us see how the failure of egoism offers some positive insight into the place morality can occupy. The egoist fails satisfactorily to resolve strategy–payoff conflicts. I have characterized the disposition needed for such resolution as conditionally cooperative. Cooperation is more than mere coordination; the cooperator selects a course of action promoting mutual benefit and adheres to it against the temptation of individually advantageous defection. Thus cooperation requires a real measure of constraint. If we relate morality to the disposition to cooperate, then moral theory will be, or at least will include, that part of the theory of rational choice that is concerned with the formulation of principles for cooperative interaction. These principles perform the traditional constraining role of morality in such a way that their rationality must be recognized by all those who, sharing the egoist's view of value and reason, realize the self-defeating character of his choices.

In the Prisoners' Dilemma the selection of cooperative strategies is unproblematic. But this is not generally true in strategy–payoff conflict. In the Dilemma there is but one plausible way of cooperating, for there is but one outcome that is both Pareto-optimal and mutually advantageous in comparison with the equilibrium outcome of egoistic behaviour. But in most strategy–payoff conflicts there are many ways of cooperating — many outcomes that are both optimal and superior for each person to what she could expect were each to seek directly to maximize value. Moral principles must enable us to select among these possibilities. If they are to be used effectively as an alternative to general egoism, then they must be reasonably simple and clearly established in accepted social practices and institutions. Cooperation depends on the ability of each cooperator to anticipate the choices of her fellows, and this is possible in general only if those choices reflect widely shared principles.

We should expect moral principles for mutually beneficial cooperation to require such traditional virtues as truth-telling and promise-keeping, as honesty, gratitude, and reciprocal benevolence. But we should not expect all of traditional morality to pass the scrutiny imposed by the cooperative standpoint. In relating morality to rational choice we seek to derive principles independent of any appeal to established practice. We are not concerned with reflective equilibrium.[35] Although it would be surprising, did no commonly recognized moral constraints relate to mutually beneficial cooperation, yet traditional morality as such may be no more than a ragbag of views lacking any single, coherent rationale. My account of morality does not attempt to refine our ordinary views, but rather to provide constraint with a firm foundation in rational choice.

7. The role of moral theory is to provide a reflective and critical standard by which existing moral practices may be assessed and revised. The standard for this reflection and criticism is provided by the individual who asks herself what she may rationally put in the place of an egoistic principle — what principle of choice, if adhered to by everyone, would be acceptable to her. And she must consider not only herself but everyone else; since her adherence to the principle is to be conditional on her expectation of others' adherence, she must expect those others also to be convinced of its acceptability.

Each person prefers to cooperate with others on terms as advantageous to herself as possible. But each must recognize that everyone has this preference. And so no one can expect others, insofar as they are rational, to accept terms of cooperation less advantageous than the least advantageous terms she herself will will accept. The recognition of mutual rationality leads to the requirement that moral principles be mutually acceptable.

---

[35] For the claim that moral theory is concerned with reflective equilibrium, see *A Theory of Justice*, pp. 20–21, 48–51.

Schematically we may represent the question of determining a mutually acceptable principle for cooperative choice in the following way. Let C be the set of feasible principles, and assume that the egoistic principle e is a member of C. Let each person i define an interval measure v_i representing the value to her of each member of C; thus for any principle p belonging to C, $v_i(p)$ is i's evaluation of p. Let $v(p)$ be the set of all individual evaluations $v_i(p)$; we shall call it the *value-representation* of p. And let $V(C)$ be the set of all value-representations $v(p)$; in other words:

$$V(C) = \{v(p): p \text{ is a member of } C\}$$
$$v(p) = \{v_i(p): i \text{ is a person}\}.$$

Now the acceptability of a principle of cooperative choice depends first on its affording each person greater expected value than does egoism. Beyond this, we may suppose that its acceptability must depend on comparing individual evaluations of the principle with evaluations of its alternatives. In other words, our problem is to select a principle r on the basis of its value-representation $v(r)$, in relation to the members of the set of value-representations $V(C)$, and the particular requirement that for each individual i, $v_i(r)$ is greater than $v_i(e)$, which we may write as: $v(r)$ is greater than $v(e)$. But this problem is isomorphic with the usual formulation of the bargaining problem in game theory: to determine an outcome, defined in terms of its values, as a point of mutual agreement, given a set of possible outcomes and a fixed outcome representing no-agreement.[36]

In section 2 of the first part I distinguished my view of the relation between rational choice and moral theory from that held by John Rawls. I claimed that moral principles are principles *for* choice, used to select among possible actions or strategies, whereas Rawls treats the principles of justice as objects *of* choice. And I claimed also that moral principles relate to strategic rationality,

---

[36] For an account of the bargaining problem, see R. D. Luce and H. Raiffa, *Games and Decisions* (New York: Wiley, 1957), pp. 124–26.

and so to situations in which each person chooses on the basis of
his expectations of others' choices, whereas Rawls relates the principles of justice to the solution of a problem of parametric rationality in which the circumstances of choice are treated as uncertain but fixed. We may now see that the distinction between
my view and that of Rawls is somewhat more complex than I
previously suggested. Moral principles are indeed principles *for*
choice, and for strategic choice. They are principles for choice in
cooperation. But they are also objects of choice, in that moral
principles would be *agreed to* by rational persons, considering
possible alternatives to the egoistic principle for situations in
which strategy–payoff conflict makes cooperation desirable. They
are the principles for choice that would be chosen by all rational
persons in situations in which everyone's choosing on the basis of
an egoistic principle would be harmful to everyone.

But if moral principles are objects of choice as well as principles for choice, note that they are not the objects of a parametric
choice. I have argued that the problem of selecting moral principles is isomorphic to the bargaining problem, and this is one of
the central questions in the theory of strategic choice. It seems to
me extraordinary that given the role of moral principles in interaction, those theorists who have wanted to relate moral theory
to the theory of rational choice, such as John Rawls and John
Harsanyi, have not recognized that the theory of bargaining, of
strategic agreement, offers the appropriate point of linkage.[37]

In proposing that we consider moral principles as the outcome
of a rational bargain, I am not suggesting that morality is a matter
of bargaining skills, as these are ordinarily understood. No doubt
the principles that would result were actual persons to negotiate
among themselves would reflect the differing abilities of the persons and the initial advantages or disadvantages that each would

---

[37] Rawls does argue for his focus on individual decision rather than bargaining
in section 20 of *A Theory of Justice*. Harsanyi never considers that ethics and bargaining might be related.

bring to the bargaining table. But although moral principles are of course to be applied by actual persons in their real interactions with their fellows, the bargain by which I suppose them selected is not itself actual. We must abstract from the real situation of actual individuals in two important ways. First, since the principles chosen are to be used as a standard for assessing social practices and institutions, they must be chosen from a position *prior* to the existing social structure. Individuals are to be thought of as choosing principles for their interaction *ex ante*, so that they can not bargain from the particular advantages or disadvantages that the actual workings of society have conferred upon them. Each may bring only his or her natural assets to the bargaining table. And second, the choice of principles is to be determined by the requirement of bargaining theory rather than by actual negotiation among imperfectly rational actors, so that each person is in effect represented at the bargaining table by an ideally rational self, and no question of differential bargaining skills arises. Moral principles are those to which our rational selves would agree, *ex ante*, for the regulation of our cooperative interactions.

Ideally rational selves do not, however, exist behind a Rawlsian veil of ignorance. Rationality here, as throughout my argument, is instrumental. Each person's rational self is fully informed about his or her abilities and interests. Thus the idea of a bargain satisfies the condition, stated but not in my view observed by John Rawls, that moral theory "take seriously the distinction between persons." [38] A rational bargain is rational from the standpoint of each person party to it; the bargain determining moral principles is thus *ex ante* rational for every person. The demand that moral theory be part of the theory of rational choice keeps the individual, not simply as a free and equal moral person,[39] but in all the richness of her talents and interests, her capa-

---

[38] *A Theory of Justice*, p. 27.

[39] The phrase "free and equal moral person" comes from Rawls; it constitutes one of the central themes of "Kantian Constructivism in Moral Theory," *Journal of Philosophy* 77 (1980), pp. 515–72.

cities and concerns, her distinctness from her fellows, as the focal point of morality.

8. And so I claim that our argument vindicates morality by appealing directly to each one of us. Not only does each of us do better by disposing himself or herself to conditional cooperation with others, but the terms of that cooperation are determined by an agreement to which each of us is fully party. Each of us may then begin as an egoist, seeking to do as well for himself or herself as possible, and supposing that this maximizing objective must guide each choice, each action. But the argument I have sketched in these lectures should lead us out of egoism; without abandoning the objective of doing as well for oneself as possible, each of us must recognize that the direct translation of that objective into a principle of choice is self-defeating. The morality of conditional cooperation offers the correct translation of the egoist's objective into action.

So what should an egoist do? Why, he should become a cooperator and consent to morality. Here I have only begun the task of illuminating that morality by an appeal to the theory of rational choice. My principle task in these papers has been a preliminary one — to sketch the incompleat egoist so that, in seeing what he lacks, we might better be able to seek out the compleat moralist.

Scientific Literacy as a Goal in a High-Technology Society

HERBERT A. SIMON

THE TANNER LECTURES ON HUMAN VALUES

Delivered at
The University of Michigan

November 11, 1983

HERBERT A. SIMON's research has ranged from computer science to psychology, administration, and economics. The thread of continuity through all of his work has been his interest in human decision-making and problem-solving processes and the implications of these processes for social institutions. In the past twenty-five years, he has made extensive use of the computer as a tool for both simulating human thinking and augmenting it with artificial intelligence.

Professor Simon was educated in political science at the University of Chicago. He has held research and faculty positions at the University of California (Berkeley), Illinois Institute of Technology, and, since 1949, Carnegie-Mellon University, where he is Richard King Mellon University Professor of Computer Science and Psychology. His writings include, among others, collections of his papers in psychology and philosophy of science, economics, and the structure of complex systems. The latest book, with K. Anders Ericsson, *Protocol Analysis*, is a continuation of their well-known article "Verbal Reports as Data."

There is a great concern in our society today, reminiscent of the post-Sputnik era, about education in science, technology, and mathematics. The concern is both about the adequacy of our supply of competent professionals trained in science and technology and the scientific "literacy" of The Celebrated Mensch in the Street, T. C. Mits.[1] Innumerable national committees and commissions, on one of which I served recently, have been appointed to examine these problems, and to recommend the actions that are required to give science and mathematics their proper place in the scheme of education. School districts across the land are reexamining their science and mathematics curricula, the competence of their teachers of these subjects, and the access of their students to microcomputers.

In my remarks here, I should like to address just one segment of the whole problem of education in science, mathematics, and technology, in particular, the concern with T. C. Mits, who does not intend to become a scientist or an engineer, but who looks forward to a long life in a high-technology society. What does Mits really need to know about scientific and technical subjects? What are the possibilities of Mits learning what he or she needs to know? I will begin with an overview of these two questions and then proceed to elaborate several aspects of them that seem to require more thorough exploration.

---

[1] T. C. Mits was the hero of the popular books on science and mathematics written some years ago by Lillian Lieber, the best-known of which was *The Education of T. C. Mits* (New York: The Galois Institute Press, 1942). I have borrowed Mr. Mits for my purposes here, altering slightly the translation of the acronym. Since a Mensch may be either a Herr or a Frau, I interpret the initial in T. C. Mits' surname in this sexless fashion.

THE NEED TO KNOW

One more discussion in general terms of the goals of education is unlikely to contribute very much to the mass of wisdom and foolishness that has already been uttered on this subject. Hence, I will not strive for novelty, but simply set forth in commonplace terms the usual taxonomy of educational objectives for T. C. Mits. In my version of that taxonomy, we should consider the needs of Mits for knowledge and skills for survival in the everyday world, the needs for knowledge and skills to which so-called liberal education is directed, and, finally, Mits' needs for adequately discharging the obligations of citizenship.

EDUCATION FOR EVERYDAY LIVING

The Mits family lives surrounded by the usual assemblage of high-tech and low-tech artifacts, although it has not yet acquired a personal computer. An investigator could follow the family through its everyday life, taking note of its interactions with these artifacts and the scientific and technical knowledge it applies in using them. Such an investigation would result in one of two conclusions, depending on the definition of "scientific and technical knowledge that was used."

When Mr. Mits cooks the family dinner (his chore on Thursdays and Saturdays), he must know how to light the stove and how to operate the can opener (which is manual, not electric). The scientific law that governs the stove is that if he turns counterclockwise the valve marked "left front," the left front burner will ignite. He must know this and many other scientific laws and facts of a similar kind. Mits and his wife are considering acquiring a new computer-controlled stove. Then they will have to assimilate additional scientific knowledge, that is, how to program such a device.

But these pieces of information and skill appear to be radically unrelated to what is usually taught in courses on physics or chemistry. In such courses, the Mitses would learn that certain inflammable gasses ignite in the presence of oxygen and combine with that oxygen to form a new compound. They might also learn that water vaporizes when heated to 100 degrees Celsius. None of that knowledge, or the much deeper knowledge they would acquire about atoms and chemical bonds and the like would really be called on very often — if ever — as they went about their everyday tasks.

Sometimes we express the distinction I am making as a difference between knowing how to work something and knowing how and why it works. Clearly, the T. C. Mits family needs to know *how to work* many artifacts, some of them quite complex and even high-tech. The repairmen they summon periodically must know *how these artifacts work*, so that they can put them into proper operating condition, or at least identify the defective modules that must be replaced. But only the designers of the artifacts and the scientists who study the natural laws employed in them feel obligated to know *why they work*.

If knowledge of how to work things is taken as the criterion of scientific and technical literacy, then the people of our society are fabulously literate — almost all of them. For better or worse, ninety-five per cent of the adults among us are licensed to operate complex and lethal motor vehicles. Yet little if any of this knowledge and skill, except perhaps the skill of reading traffic signs, is acquired through formal education. You will immediately confront me with the counterexample of driver education courses. I will respond by questioning whether such courses serve any essential educational purpose, since generations of drivers, including my own, learned without them.

Moreover, it is an interesting question, whose answer is not at all obvious, whether those of us who are trained in science or engineering are any more skillful in handling artifacts than is the T. C. Mits family. Are engineers especially good automobile drivers? And are their diets more nutritious than those of persons who majored in English literature?

However, I really do not want to engage in a discussion as to whether courses in driver education, nutrition, and personal hygiene should be taught in the schools. The point is that if there is some illiteracy in these matters, it is not irremediable. And in any event, it is not this ignorance that we have in mind when we talk about scientific illiteracy.

The conclusion we reach is that scientific literacy is neither a necessary nor a sufficient condition for our everyday interactions with our artifacts. We can dismiss this aspect of the education of T. C. Mits and family from our consideration.

LIBERAL EDUCATION

Since I do not anticipate much success in defining either the term "liberal education" or the goals that such education is intended to reach, I will not even attempt a rigorous characterization. Instead, I shall try to establish some outer and inner limits of what liberal education might encompass, with the hope that such vague indications may satisfy our needs for definition.

In particular, I should like to avoid puzzling over whether liberal education is supposed to be useful or not. Utility itself is a slippery concept. In the framework of traditional Christianity, education is useful if it contributes to the salvation of the soul and not very useful otherwise. Alternative pictures of the human condition lead to other definitions of utility.

In the writing on liberal education there does seem to be some consensus that it has to do with the cultivation of the "whole person," and that such cultivation may be expected to have (beneficial) consequences for the fullness of life and the level of morality that life attains. The concerns of liberal education, as usually defined, tend to be speciescentric. The human condition, including both the existential problem that every person faces and the problems of interaction among human beings, has a central place in these concerns — a humanistic concern complementing or replacing the theological concerns that I mentioned previously.

The relation of human beings to their natural environment has played, historically, a much smaller role in conceptions of liberal education. This, of course, was the complaint of C. P. Snow in his "Two Cultures" argument, and I share Snow's views on this matter.[2] Let me explain briefly why I think his views are correct.

The phrase "natural philosophy" symbolizes the relation that has long been perceived between the questions that human beings ask about their own existence and some of the basic questions of the natural sciences. In fact, the connection is so close that the four fields of greatest excitement in basic science today are also the fields that are most relevant to questions about the meaning of life: What is matter? What is the origin and fate of the cosmos? What is life? What is mind?

1. *What is matter?* The pursuit of this question is the task of particle physics, armed with ever more powerful accelerators. I suppose that there are few who believe that the quest can ever lead to final answers, but the interminability of the effort does not dull the imperative urge to continue the search into deeper and deeper recesses of the world of elementary particles.

2. *What is the origin and fate of the cosmos?* Answering this question, closely related to the first one, is the task today of astrophysics, armed with space vehicles, radio telescopes, and the sharp tools of mathematical physics. Here, too, the finality of answers is elusive.

3. *What is life?* Here the powerful methods of contemporary molecular biology lead us ever closer to a reduction, at least an "in principle" reduction, of the laws governing living organisms to the laws of chemistry and physics.

4. *What is mind?* Jurisdiction over this question has only in recent times been transferred from the domain of philosophy to that of cognitive science, which now has available the modern computer as a powerful tool of investigation, indispensable for both simulation of mind and formalization of theories about it.

<hr>

[2] C. P. Snow, *The Two Cultures and the Scientific Revolution* (Cambridge: Cambridge University Press, 1959).

Particle physics, astrophysics, molecular biology, and cognitive science provide us today with our creation myths, to replace those pre-scientific ones that no longer satisfy us. And we feel a profound need for these creation myths in contemplating our place in the universe and the nature of the human condition. Whatever may have been the case five hundred years ago, there can be no question today that science is an essential component of liberal education. Snow was quite right in questioning whether one who did not understand the Second Law of Thermodynamics could think the thoughts of an educated person.

There is more to humanism than the question of mankind's relation to nature, or even the existential question. To the list of central questions, we must add, at least:

> 5. *How do we know about the external world?* The epistemological question, closely associated with the nature of mind, is also, today, a central focus of inquiry in cognitive science.

> 6. *What is the relation of motivation and emotion to thought?* Psychology must encompass the wanting and feeling person as well as the thinking person.

> 7. *How do human beings relate to each other?* To which we may wish to add: "and how should they?"

This is neither intended to be an exhaustive list of Big Questions nor an assertion of priorities. Rather, it is a *minimal* list of questions that are centrally relevant to liberal education and that can be addressed seriously only with the help of scientific knowledge. One might suppose this conclusion to be uncontroversial, but it is not. It is slightly paradoxical that, among the sciences, the claim of the social and behavioral sciences for an important role in liberal education is sometimes questioned even more vociferously than the claim of the physical and biological sciences. In fact, if the latter sciences did not sometimes have mathematical content and were not generally "hard" (in the pedagogical meaning of that term), it is likely that all of the opposition to science in the liberal arts curriculum would be focused on the social sciences.

The paradox is really not so hard to understand. For the social sciences and the humanities are direct competitors in their claims to special possession of the wisdom that is relevant to at least the last three of the questions I have listed. "Does one learn more about human nature by reading Shakespeare or a psychology textbook?" The reader's answer to the question will disclose which culture commands his loyalty. Having raised the question, I intend to leave it open. In a recent lecture, I have made some brief suggestions about how to approach an answer.[3] For the moment, I would be satisfied if we could agree that the human condition can be illuminated by literature, by history, by philosophy, by the arts, and by the social and behavioral sciences as well. (If I have left out your favorite subject, I shall be glad to add it to the list.)

In the preceding paragraphs, I have sketched out the claims of science, both natural and social, to relevance for many of the topics which have always had an important place in the liberal curriculum. But the concerns that have been addressed so far do not by any means cover all of the goals that have usually been proposed for liberal education. I should like now to turn to the goal of preparing students for the responsibilities of citizenship.

EDUCATION FOR CITIZENSHIP

If people do not need scientific knowledge to drive their cars or cook their meals, do they need it to cast their ballots wisely, or to write intelligent letters to their legislators? That there is an enormous technical component in the assessment of many or most public policy questions today is obvious. The consequences of setting automobile emission standards tighter or looser than they now are depend on the chemical processes in internal combustion engines, the chemistry of the atmosphere (with a little meteorol-

[3] *Reason in Human Affairs* (Palo Alto: Stanford University Press, 1983), pp. 29–34.

ogy mixed in), human physiological responses to contaminants in
air, and the social and economic costs of illness and death. All of
these matters are subjects of scientific inquiry, some in the physical
sciences, others in the biological sciences, and still others in the
social sciences.

Even policy issues that do not seem as obviously "technical"
as this one are heavily impregnated with questions of fact, the
answers to which are likely to be determined reliably only on the
basis of scientific inquiry. One of the central and perennial issues
in societies throughout history has been to arrive at an appropriate balance between providing incentives to socially productive
effort and preserving some measure of equality in the distribution
of the social product among families and individuals. Our view
of this balance will depend very strongly on whether we think that
we can provide effective incentives without accepting substantial
inequality. In our time we have seen two immense nations, the
Russian and the Chinese, try to fashion a New Man who would
give his best efforts in production without differential reward.
Most of us, perhaps including most of the people in those nations,
are unimpressed with the success of the experiments. But the
shifting economic policies we see pursued in these and other countries are perhaps far less a reflection of shifting values than of
shifting beliefs and expectations about the laws of human behavior. Social science is as relevant to the question as ethics.

We must not be hasty in concluding, from this and the many
similar examples we could adduce, that T. C. Mits needs to know
a great deal of science in order to be a responsible citizen. The
important thing is not that *Mits* be able to supply the correct
factual premises for making these decisions, but that the correct
premises be supplied, somehow, by the political process. If we
could hire experts to give us the facts, just as we hire doctors and
auto mechanics to deal with the technical facts of everyday life,
we could spare ourselves a technical education as a condition for
citizenship. In this respect the citizenship argument for scientific

literacy is a less compelling argument than the arguments of the last section which rested on human needs for philosophical understanding of their world.

I will return in a later section of my remarks to the educational requirements for citizenship. We cannot reach a conclusion on this matter until we inquire into the feasibility of attaining widespread scientific literacy, and until we have examined possible alternative political arrangements that would eliminate or reduce the need for it. I will take up the topic of feasibility after I have commented on one other matter: the incompatibility that is sometimes supposed to exist between liberal and vocational, or liberal and useful, education.

LIBERAL VERSUS VOCATIONAL

Historically, resistance to the replacement of traditional by scientific subjects in the curriculum has been based on the idea that scientific and technical knowledge, as contrasted with liberal knowledge, is *merely* useful. Of course, the argument cannot be intended quite literally; the contrast cannot be between useful and useless, but between those things that are useful only to "practical" ends and those that are useful to more fundamental and important ones.

The argument rests on a premise that needs to be questioned. That premise is that scientific subjects are (ought to be?) mainly taught to produce and develop skills, while liberal subjects are taught to produce understanding. Understanding is a requirement for the liberally educated person; skill is not.

Of course, postulating an incompatibility between skill and understanding is nonsense — for more than one reason. First, it is improbable that any but the narrowest skill can be imparted without imparting some measure of understanding. In most circumstances, learning "why" greatly facilitates learning "how to," and facilitates, also, retaining what one learns. If the skill involves a highly repetitive action, performed in an unchanging way from one week to the next, then understanding may contribute little to the quality of the performance. But in a constantly changing environment, skill must be modified continually and transferred to new situations. And there is ample evidence that skill without understanding of underlying principles simply does not transfer.

This is hardly a novel argument. It has been used for decades, if not centuries, to distinguish between the education appropriate to "technicians" (skills without understanding) and "professionals" (understanding with some skill). Today we would probably insist that the technician, too, will not long retain useful skills without an understanding that is sufficient to adapt them to continually changing applications.

A second objection to contrasting skill with understanding is that almost all genuine understanding contains a large component of skill. To understand a foreign language (an accomplishment traditionally within the scope of liberal education) means acquiring the skills of reading, writing, speaking, and listening to it, or some subset of these. To understand literature means acquiring the skills of extracting meanings from prose, of extracting ideas from it, of comparing and contrasting ideas, of attending to the beauty of language, of assessing and judging character, of forming mental images, and many others.

A liberal subject, taught effectively, teaches skills. And a vocational subject, taught fundamentally, teaches understanding. The fact that there are skills based on science, technology, and mathematics says nothing about the relevance of these subjects to liberal education, or the understanding that can be acquired by studying them.

THE FEASIBILITY OF PRODUCING SCIENTIFIC LITERACY

Necessity is alleged to be the mother of invention, but no human necessity has yet produced a gravity shield. It may be questioned on the same ground whether the importance of scientific literacy to a society, or to the individuals in it, is a sufficient cause to produce that literacy or even to guarantee its possibility. There may be no way from here to there.

C. P. Snow observed, correctly, that in our society some measure of literacy in language, literature, and the arts is expected of every "educated" person, but that even an elementary literacy in science and mathematics beyond arithmetic (perhaps we should say, beyond addition and subtraction) is not. The "educated" person is also expected to be able to discuss public affairs and to exhibit a certain amount of information about them, but his discussion of them need not be informed by any systematic training in the social sciences. These are the asymmetries between humanistic and scientific education that Snow deplores in his "Two Cultures" essay.

Presumably this could all be changed, if we thought it wrong, simply by changing the curriculum of primary, secondary, and college education to require of everyone a larger measure of scientific study. But can it be changed? Snow points to a second interesting social phenomenon. Not only are many people innocent of scientific knowledge, and not only are they unembarrassed about admitting this deficiency, but they are often heard to proclaim, "I never was able to understand math [or physics, or organic chemistry, or economics]."

Now if a society's attitudes toward education changed, so would these habits of speech. People would become private know-nothings instead of proclaiming publicly their ignorance of science and mathematics. But the worrisome possibility is that perhaps they are telling the truth; that they *could not* learn these subjects even in the face of strong social pressures to do so.

A SCIENCE–MATHEMATICS BUMP?

The Two Hemispheres. The hypothesis is rather popular nowadays that there are two distinct kinds of intelligence: the analytic intelligence of scientific and technical thinking, supposed to be localized in the left hemisphere of the brain (at least in right-handed people), and the intuitive, creative intelligence of non-technical thinking, which is supposed to be localized in the right hemisphere.

There is of course solid physiological evidence for some specialization of function between the two hemispheres of the brain, and, for that matter, among various subregions within each hemisphere. There is also evidence, however, of considerable relocatability of function in response to brain damage, particularly early brain damage. But brain location is largely irrelevant to the question of whether there are two quite autonomous and qualitatively different forms of thought. To say that the hemispheres are specialized is like saying that the engine of an automobile is usually in the front, while the differential is commonly in the rear. This is true of most automobiles, but it in no way implies that there are two ways in which an automobile can operate, one with the engine and one with the differential.

The important question, then, is whether or not humans (some humans) are capable of two distinct modes of thought, each carried out with a different mechanism. The fact of brain specialization may facilitate experimentation that will help answer the question, but it is not, in itself, at the heart of it. How strong is the evidence, then, for these two autonomous modes of thought? It is mainly negative.

The right hemisphere is supposed to be the principal site for visual and auditory recognition and imagery processes, but the left hemisphere is distinctly the site of most linguistic processes and linguistic knowledge, both syntactic and lexical. The pitch of a pure tone appears to be recognized by the right hemisphere, but as soon as harmony enters the picture, the left hemisphere, with its syntactic capabilities, comes into play. Thus, it would appear that the musical experience is an experience of the whole person, and not of some special holistic process ensconced in the right hemisphere. In fact, there is no solid evidence, known to me, that any single important human cognitive function can be carried out by the right hemisphere without the participation of the left. Specifically, there is no evidence that some people make "right brain" intuitive decisions, while others make "left brain" analytic decisions. The facts of hemispheric localization are much more mundane and prosaic than the romances that have been woven out of them.

Analytic and Intuitive Thought. What, then, about the common subjective experience that we attain some of our ideas and conclusions suddenly and intuitively, while others are attained on the basis of sustained conscious effort and analysis? The mass of evidence for such a distinction cannot be denied, even if it could be shown conclusively that it has nothing to do with hemispheric specialization. What is important is how the difference is to be *interpreted*; in particular, what is important is to arrive at a clear scientific explanation for the process that we call intuition.

The defining conditions for intuition have already been mentioned. A problem is posed: e.g., a patient describes symptoms to a physician. Without any apparent effort, and almost immediately, the physician says, "You have chicken pox." A prudent physician will ask some further questions, make additional observations, and perhaps call for some tests before regarding the diagnosis as final. But the remarkable fact, the one that confirms our belief in the reality of intuition, is that the skillful physician's first judgment, arrived at within a minute, is usually right.

Sometimes, as in certain celebrated occasions in the annals of science — Poincaré boarding the bus at Coutances, Kekulé staring into the fire — the successful intuition is an answer to a question that has long been pursued, without success, and that has temporarily been laid aside. Except for these circumstances of preparation and "incubation," the phenomenological signs of intuition are just like those of the more prosaic and frequent occasions of professional practice. The central phenomenon is that the expert can often know without conscious sustained thought.

When it is stated in this way, the frequency with which experts exhibit intuition should occasion little surprise — no more surprise than that Mits can usually recognize his wife instantly (i.e., within a second or so) when she approaches him on the street, even if he is not expecting to see her there. Not only does he recognize her, but all sorts of information about her, stored in memory during the course of a long marriage, becomes available to him. The capacity for intuitions is the capacity for recognizing familiar situations, old acquaintances, on the basis of perceptual cues that present themselves, and for evoking from memory information that one has stored about the recognized situations. The intuitive brain is simply the expert brain, and intuitions occur no less frequently in the practice of the sciences and technical professions than they do in the arts and humanities.

If we describe thought that requires more than intuition, and that is conscious and sustained, as "analytic" thought, then we would expect to find greater or lesser amounts of analytic thought admixed with greater or lesser amounts of intuition in all kinds of intellectual performances. But we should be surprised to find any considerable sequence of expert thinking that was not liberally sprinkled with intuitions. Moreover, such evidence as we have of creative thinking in the sciences and the arts indicates that analytic and intuitive thinking go on side by side in both. If there is a "mathematics bump" in the brain, or a "literature bump," or any other, it appears unlikely that its presence or absence is much associated with a preference for intuitive or analytic thinking, or a differential capacity for the one or the other.

Math and Science Aptitude. Dismissing the analytic–intuitive dichotomy, however, does not dispose of the question of whether there may be a substantial number of people who, though exhibiting high levels of intelligence on tests of verbal ability, are yet unable to acquire skills in science, and especially science requiring the use of mathematics. The fact that there are demonstrably many people who do fail in science and mathematics, and who find courses in these subjects exceedingly painful and impenetrable, does not prove the point one way or another. There is always the alternative explanation of motivation, of the primary school teacher who successfully immunized students against ever enjoying mathematics or succeeding in it. Perhaps what we are dealing with is not a cognitive inadequacy but trauma. That is certainly a tenable hypothesis, but we should not be too quick to embrace it until we have a much deeper factual understanding of the situation than we now have.

One curious fact, though it is a fact supported only by anecdotal evidence, is that for persons with high verbal aptitude but low mathematical aptitude, their difficulties with mathematics are most acute when they face tasks that require translation between verbal and mathematical representations of information. Middle school algebra teachers report, for example, that most students of good general ability master the mechanics of manipulating algebraic expressions. The moment of truth — the moment that separates those who will continue in science and mathematics from those who will leave the arena as soon as they are permitted to — arrives when the students are confronted with their first algebra story problems, problems stated in natural language that has to be translated into the language of equations. One might naïvely suppose that this would be precisely the part of the algebra course in which students of high verbal ability would shine. If the anecdotes are reliable, it is not.

In setting goals of scientific and mathematical literacy, it would seem to be of utmost importance to understand the nature of the difficulties I have just described and the prospects for alleviating them. To acquire that understanding, we have to analyze deeply the processes that are involved in performing such tasks as solving algebra word problems or physics problems. Some of the research in cognitive psychology of the past several decades has already given us important hints as to what these processes are.[4] Let me use an analogy to explain what has been learned. A skilled translator putting a French text into English does not make a direct syntactical-cum-lexical translation from the source language to the target. Moreover, mechanical translation schemes that attempt to do just that have been uniformly disappointing and unsuccessful. What the expert translator does is to extract the meaning from the French text, transposing it into some kind of internal "semantic" representation, and only then rendering that semantic representation into English in the same way that English prose is generated from internal thoughts. Observation of students who have difficulties with word problems in algebra and physics has frequently revealed that they are unsuccessful in translating the natural language of the problem description into an adequate semantic representation. Their difficulties appear to center less upon the mathematical symbolism than on creating a mental representation to which that symbolism can be applied.

On the basis of any evidence of which I am aware, it is simply unknown whether and by what means these difficulties can be overcome. I do not even know what probabilities to assign to the possibilities. To the extent that math-blindness and science-blindness are incorrigible, we shall have to limit our goals of universal literacy. The consequences could be serious, for we could be continuing to exclude a portion of the population from a feeling of full participation in the affairs of our high-technology society. That feeling of exclusion is not uncommonly accompanied by alienation from the society, or at least hostility toward its technologies and a feeling of helplessness about them. Both are significantly present in our own and other high-technology societies today.

---

[4] See J. Larkin, J. McDermott, D. P. Simon, and H. A. Simon, "Expert and novice performance in solving physics problems," *Science* 208 (1980), pp. 1335–42, and references cited there.

It seems highly unlikely that unsusceptibility to science and mathematics education is an all-or-none matter. Hence, there is no reason to postpone our efforts to raise the general level of literacy until such time as we have accurate knowledge of the limits. Activities aimed at raising literacy and efforts aimed at understanding the difficulties encountered along the way can go hand in hand.

To the extent that we regard scientific literacy to be an important goal for a high-technology society, or for any society, we need to assign a correspondingly high priority to research aimed at gaining a deeper understanding of the nature of the internal representations that are effective in solving problems in domains like physics and chemistry, the nature of the individual differences in aptitude for constructing such representations from problem descriptions, and the means for improving those aptitudes, particularly among those in whom they are weak. Until we have such an understanding, and preferably also an understanding of what methods are effective for improving this skill, it will be hard to define realistic social goals for literacy.

We need this understanding not only for the students of science, but for the teachers as well. There is much concern today as to whether all or most of the teachers responsible for science instruction in the schools, particularly at the elementary level, themselves have the depth of understanding of science and mathematics that is needed for effective instruction in these subjects.

COMPUTER LITERACY

In recent discussion of school curricula, the topic of computer literacy has assumed an even greater prominence than literacy in science and mathematics. We need to ask just what the connection is between these two kinds of literacy, for it is not at all obvious. We may be interested in providing students with the skills necessary in using a computer, in helping them to understand mathematics by using the computer as an instructional device, or in using the computer as a tool for instruction in science. These are different things.

In their ability to assume an active role in interaction with their users, computers are unlike any of our previous artifacts. Domestic animals are the closest analogy, and they cannot speak. The level of sophistication that can be reached in human interaction with computers has little or nothing to do with the hardware but depends instead on programming. And since our experience with computers is very limited — only a generation, and that devoted mainly to number-crunching — we have hardly begun to realize the potential of computers as active partners in an educational process.

Because of the limits on human imagination in dealing with novel complexities, the first generation of computer-aided instruction systems has (with some notable exceptions) largely been limited to using the computer as a substitute for a programmed textbook, providing massive opportunity for drill and practice. Drill and practice programs have a useful place in instruction, but they are not at all what CAI will mean in the future. As research in artificial intelligence advances, we will find ways to provide computers with more and more of the capabilities of an intelligent human tutor, and perhaps other capabilities as well. At what point and to what extent we will be able to afford to use these capabilities for instruction on a large scale is harder to foresee. And we must continue to give equal attention to the ways open to us, with or without computers, for raising the competence of our human teaching force.

Computers Teaching Computing. Let me turn now to the various applications of computers to instruction in computation. Computer literacy in the narrowest sense is the easiest to comprehend. The main precondition for automobile "literacy" in our society was the widespread availability of automobiles. In the same way, the wide availability of computers is the necessary, and almost sufficient, condition for computer literacy. "Literacy" in its narrowest sense means the ability to use computers in simple applications like arithmetic calculation and word processing. These can be taught and learned as rather narrow skills and with little or no understanding of the computer hardware or software that implements them.

I suppose that by computer literacy we usually mean, or should mean, somewhat more than this. The most ambitious attempt to use the computer to teach basic concepts of computation — in particular, to lead users to an understanding of the fundamental notion of *procedure* — has been the activity associated with the programming language LOGO. The efforts of Seymour Papert and his associates to apply LOGO to education from the earliest levels have been as imaginative as the language itself. However, we do not yet have systematic evaluations of the educational impact of LOGO on students. We do not know what is learned, how effectively it is learned, or what individual differences may be expected in the response to systems of this kind. Nevertheless, I think a good case can be made for LOGO-like approaches to computer literacy in contrast to standard instruction in programming in languages like BASIC or FORTRAN.

The goal is to make the computer, for T. C. Mits, a less mysterious and magical object than it has been; to provide all or most of us with some insight into how it is able to do all kinds of things that resemble the things that we humans can do by thinking. And if that insight can be provided, it will carry with it a considerable insight into how the human mind works, penetrating that mystery also.

Computers Teaching Science. So much for the "egocentric" use of computers to teach about themselves. They also offer much promise, although a promise largely unrealized, to contribute to the teaching of mathematics and science. We can already catch a few glimpses of the directions that such instruction may take. For twenty-five years, a number of graduate schools of business have been using computerized business games to give students the experience of making decisions in realistic manufacturing, marketing, and financial environments. For nearly the same length of time, some students in chemistry, genetics, and psychology (and perhaps many other subjects) have been provided with data banks that allow them to plan, run, and interpret simulated experiments. As graphic display devices have become more widely available, computerized displays have been applied to teaching about various kinds of dynamic systems, giving students an opportunity to visualize the changes in dynamic behavior that result from altering system parameters. Students in history and sociology courses have been provided with data banks that allow them to test empirically some of the theses they find asserted in their textbooks. Programs that diagnose student errors, and work interactively with the student to remove them, are under development for subjects ranging from arithmetic and electronics to writing.

We can look forward to at least a generation of rapid exploration of these potential applications of the computer to education, and at the end of that generation (and possibly long before) the label CAI will have a radically changed meaning. What is less certain is whether the computer has any special contribution to make to the problem discussed in the previous section: whether it can help reduce the number of people who are immune to instruction in scientific mathematical subjects. I hesitate to make a prediction, one way or the other.

A Closer Look at Science and Citizenship

I have already introduced the topic of the needs of scientific education for effective citizenship and raised the question whether access to experts could substitute for literacy. I should now like to turn the question around: Would literacy be an adequate substitute for access to experts? Let me take as a difficult example the policy decisions we have to make in our society about energy sources.

Every discussion of energy policy today encompasses not only the questions of exhaustibility of resources but also the vexing issues of environmental effects of using one source of energy or another. Petroleum, nuclear energy, coal, biomass, gasified coal, and solar energy are all claimants for a major role in the supply of our energy. Understanding each of these sources and its environmental implications involves a formidable body of physics, chemistry, meteorology, geology, physiology, and perhaps other sciences as well.

We are concerned with the disposal of slow-decaying nuclear wastes. What do we know about the capacities of deep-lying salt deposits for containing such wastes in the long run? Some of our fuel sources produce immense quantities of carbon dioxide, which is vented to the atmosphere. What is the magnitude of the greenhouse effect, and what is the time scale within which we need to be concerned about it? What are the economics and ergonomics of the production of biomass for fuel? Can we obtain it without consuming more energy for fertilizer and cultivation than we harvest for fuel? What are the prospects for storing large enough amounts of solar energy to tide over periods of nighttime and overcast? What are the prospects of achieving economical energy production from nuclear fusion, and what kinds of wastes will be produced from fusion processes? What are the prospects and costs of extracting the sulfur oxides that produce acid rain from the stack gasses of coal plants?

This is just a sample of the questions that can be asked about energy policy. No matter how great our enthusiasm for educating the Mits family in science and technology, it is unlikely that they will ever feel confident in their abilities to handle these questions without expert help. And where are the experts? Even if the Mitses can find experts to answer *each* of these questions (a matter to which I will return in a moment), they are highly unlikely to encounter many who can answer *all* of them. Even if they can get answers, how are they to put them all together?

CAN WE LEAVE IT TO THE EXPERTS?

By an expert on some topic, we mean someone who knows all that is known about it and can reason correctly about that knowledge. What is known, however, may not be enough to answer the Mitses' questions, or ours. Today, it is generally agreed among atmospheric scientists that an increase in carbon dioxide in the atmosphere will cause a warming of the earth's climate. Less than fifteen years ago, I heard several of the country's principal experts discuss this topic. They all agreed that carbon dioxide in the atmosphere had three, additive, effects upon temperature. One was the greenhouse effect, and I have forgotten the nature of the other two. The greenhouse effect had a positive sign (more CO_2, higher temperature), while the other two had negative signs (more CO_2, lower temperatures). However, understanding of the processes was not then complete enough to determine whether the positive or negative signs dominated. That was the most expert opinion available, but it was cold comfort to anyone responsible for recommending policy. Today we are better off. It seems to be agreed that the positive term dominates. But experts can still disagree widely as to the magnitude of the effect.

We may be tempted to dismiss this problem as irrelevant to scientific literacy. If we human beings, collectively, do not have the knowledge we need, no training in science or mathematics, and no lack of it, will remedy the situation. But if the Mitses and their friends are to use the experts wisely, they should have some capacity to judge when the experts really know and when they are guessing. A measure of scientific literacy might be exceedingly useful in assessing the degree of certainty of the scientific conclusions presented to them.

Expert advice has to be evaluated not only with respect to its certainty, but also with respect to possible biases of the experts. We are accustomed to making allowance for bias arising out of pecuniary interest, and frequently we require our experts to disclose any conflicts of financial interests they may have. We are increasingly aware of, but perhaps not yet fully sophisticated about, biases that arise from human bounded rationality. The human mind, even the brightest human mind, can only embrace a very small part of all human knowledge, and can attend at one time to only a tiny fraction of even this small part. One way it deals with these limitations is to limit the goals with which it is concerned and confine its attention to a subset of all the causal connections in the situations it is considering. And in this process of narrowing, the part on which attention focuses becomes more interesting, more important, and somehow more valuable. Hence, several years of immersion in research or development on the X energy source is highly likely to produce a deep conviction in the researcher or engineer that X is a highly desirable source of energy, that continuing research and development will certainly soon assure its technical feasibility and bring it within our means, and that its deleterious environmental effects, if any, can be reduced to acceptable proportions.

In an area of science or technology where human knowledge is relatively complete (if there are any such), we could presumably predict what an expert would tell us if we ourselves possessed the expert body of knowledge. In most areas of real complexity, like the energy technologies I have mentioned, different scientists, all expert and reasonable, could tell us quite different things. The most useful information about them, if we want to predict what they will tell us, is information about their professional histories, their identifications and commitments. If we want a favorable view of nuclear energy, we go to Edward Teller and not to Barry Commoner.

To make this observation is not to accuse these experts, or any others, of venality or mendacity. It is simply to affirm the well-known phenomenon that human rationality is severely bounded, and that identifications with particular goals, particular subject matters, particular people and groups of people, and particular regions of space and time provide some of the important boundaries that allow us to simplify problems to manageable (if unrealistic) proportions. Commitment to nuclear power or to energy from biomass arises from the same psychological sources, derives from the same psychological mechanisms, as commitment to American (or Chinese, or Russian) supremacy in science and technology. They are all corollaries to the proposition that what we know well we value and seek to perfect.

INSTITUTIONALIZING EXPERTISE

The recognition that experts operate with uncertainties that are sometimes immense and identify with partial viewpoints that are inescapably blinding leads to a variety of proposals for improving the quality of expert advice by institutionalizing the process of providing it. The National Research Council and its governing organizations, the National Academy of Sciences and the National Academy of Engineering, provide an example of such institutionalization. The function of the National Research Council is to provide expert advice, on request, to the organs of the national government, executive and legislative. A variety of mechanisms are built into the structure to guarantee the highest attainable levels of expertness and objectivity. Membership in the governing bodies is determined by a rigorous process that is supposed to weigh only scientific and technical eminence, and which probably comes about as close to this goal as human imperfections in motive and judgment allow. Membership is for life, eliminating one form of external pressure. A large part of the membership, especially of the NAS, is based in universities, which are generally perceived as more closely identified with the public interest — or at least less identified with special interests — than are most other employing institutions.

The governing group of the NAS-NAE-NRC complex selects ad hoc committees to examine the specific questions that are put before it. The selection process takes into account both expertness and the need to balance interests and prior identifications, where these are known or can be guessed. Nominees are expected to disclose conflicts of interest that might bias their judgments.

There is fairly wide agreement among persons familiar with the operation of these institutions that they perform a useful and sometimes important function, and that they are not perfect. Cries of conflict of interest have sometimes accompanied the publication of reports on controversial topics, but that is to be expected— and may even occasionally have some validity. But the most severe limitations of this use of experts are limitations of scientific and technical knowledge. On some occasions, a committee has given advice that, from hindsight, was poor. On other occasions, a committee has given advice that seemed to some to be wishy-washy. (Senator Muskie once complained that scientists were "two-handed." On the one hand, they said "yes," on the other hand, "no." In the face of uncertainties and gaps in knowledge, others might describe the same behavior as "even-handed.") When these things have occurred, I believe that they can most often be attributed to genuine inadequacies in the scientific knowledge available for answering the questions posed.

Earlier, I mentioned auto emission standards as an example of a policy question that called for extensive knowledge of science and technology. Since I once chaired an NAS committee that offered advice on this topic (to Senator Muskie!), I might say a few more words about it. In principle, the problem had a clear conceptual structure. The chain of causality ran from automobiles to chemical reactions in the atmosphere, to the air we breathe, to human health. The greatest conceptual difficulty lay in balancing costs and benefits, which clearly involved (implicitly or explicitly) assigning values to life and health that could be compared with resource costs. Any economist, and many noneconomists, could write down the equations that would formalize this conception and seek an optimal answer by equating partial derivatives, the coefficients that represented the effects of policy changes and their costs or values.

But the practical difficulty that faced the committee in reaching conclusions and recommendations lay in quite a different direction. How were we to find the actual numbers to assign to these coefficients? We had available to us the nation's experts on automobile engineering, atmospheric chemistry, cost-benefit analysis, and the health effects of toxic substances in air. Almost none of them (except the engineers) felt confident or even comfortable in providing quantitative estimates of the strengths of the causal connections that they studied. The health experts, for example, were willing to hazard judgments about the minimum concentrations of certain substances that would have toxic effects. They were most uncomfortable when asked how much these health effects would increase as the concentrations increased. Yet the latter judgments, not the former, provided the relevant parameter for the decision that had to be made.

What can you say of recommendations arrived at under these circumstances? For the committee did make recommendations. You can say, I believe, that the scientific evidence that the committee reviewed placed limits, very broad limits to be sure, on the range of conclusions and recommendations that was scientifically acceptable. You can say that the recommendations finally agreed upon by the committee were such as reasonable people, with a good understanding of the evidence, could have adopted. Whether this degree of certainty is sufficient to deal adequately with the questions that face our society is uncertain. That it is as much certainty as we are able to attain is quite evident.

EXPERTS AND T. C. MITS

Experts are used in our society through a large variety of institutional arrangements and channels, of which the NAS-NAE-NRC structure is only one example, albeit perhaps the most prominent one. Whatever the arrangements, the problems that are encountered in using them are very similar to those that I have illustrated in my example. In light of these problems, we clearly will not wish to depend on the experts alone. What additional procedures are available? In particular, what role can the Mits family play in the process?

Courts and legislatures give us models of deliberation that are alternatives to the expert process that I have described. Both of these alternatives share a couple of properties: they do not rely on experts to make the final decision, although they may call on them for assistance; and they both assume that the relevant interests will be represented in the process — to that extent, they are adversary proceedings. Both are attuned to bounded rationality and to conflict of interest. Rashomon is no stranger to them.

Even the rank layman can be informed by listening carefully to experts presenting conflicting analyses. I have observed a federal district judge hearing testimony, in a patent suit, about the physical processes that cause the arc to extinguish when an electric switch is opened. At the end of the week, he appeared to be wiser and better informed than he was at the beginning. As far as I know, he was innocent of formal training in physics, but cross-examination can be a powerful method for eliciting truth. And there would seem to be good reason to believe that Judge Mits or Attorney Mits could ask sharper and more penetrating questions about scientific and technical disputes if she had a modicum of scientific understanding of the matter at hand than if she were wholly ignorant of it.

This is the strong case for teaching science for citizenship. It is illusory to suppose that such instruction can produce expertness, even over a tiny range of the questions that face courts, legislatures, and consumers today. But it is not illusory to think that the Mits family can become more effective questioners and cross-examiners than they would be without such training.

If this is to be a primary goal of science for the citizen, we can ask what content of the science curriculum is most suitable for attaining it. At the outset, we can dismiss any great concern for subject-matter coverage, for we are not trying to produce experts;

we are trying to produce questioners and adjudicators. Since we can cover only an infinitesimal part of the subject matter that is potentially relevant, there is no part that we *must* cover. Far more important than subject matter is the method of science: the nature of scientific evidence, the ways in which that evidence is obtained, and the ways in which it can be interpreted. Of course, methodology is sterile when taught in abstraction. What needs to be taught are specific bodies of science — sampled from the whole domain — viewed and examined as instances of the application of scientific method. It is far less important what particular examples are chosen than how they are explored.

One advantage of this approach to scientific literacy is that it brings about a convergence between the goals of liberal education and the goals of producing a literate citizenry. A second advantage is that it affords some opportunity to avoid the worst difficulties of possibly incorrigible illiteracy that I addressed in the last section. Incorrigibility seems to center on subjects with a mathematical, or at least a formal, structure. We need not organize the whole curriculum around such subjects, although it would be unfortunate to avoid them altogether (allowing the "science requirement" to be satisfied by a course in anthropology or geology).

In proposing this emphasis on the methods of science, I do not believe that I am proposing a "science for poets" approach. The potential cross-examiner or questioner needs to know some science, not just something *about* science. Specifically, it is unlikely that any considerable appreciation of the scientific process or of the weight to be placed on scientific conclusions is to be gained without a student's going through that process and striving to reach such conclusions. If in the course of achieving this objective some scientific content is also learned, as it surely will be, so much the better.

Knowing Ourselves: The Social Sciences

"We have met the enemy and they is us." It is all too easy to locate the problems that face our species in the physical world that surrounds us. Their real locus is in ourselves. And one of the conditions that complicates our efforts to deal with our problems is ignorance of ourselves. Scientific literacy cannot be limited to understanding of the external world; it must encompass literacy in the sciences of man.

It may be credible to equate knowledge with power, but surely not with virtue. There is no certainty that if the Mitses understand the economy better, or the ways their brains work, or the psychological and sociological roots of racial prejudice, that they will behave in more benign ways. But there is reasonable certainty that if they continue in ignorance of these matters, they will create many problems for themselves and others. For this reason, I must give a prominent place to the social sciences in the curriculum for scientific literacy.

In teaching the social sciences, as in teaching the physical and biological sciences, coverage is not the issue. It is neither possible nor desirable for its own sake. What needs to be taught is something about the tools we have available for inquiring objectively about ourselves, as individuals and as members of families, organizations, economies, and polities. What need to be taught, also, are ways of challenging and testing the received wisdom, the proverbs about human behavior that pass in everyday discussion as explanations of human phenomena.

What we can teach goes no further than what we know. I am not one of those who think we know little, scientifically, about human behavior. The fact that economists cannot predict next year's production or fine-tune the economy does not mean that they do not have a considerable understanding of how a complex economy operates and a great deal of consensus — comparable, let us say, to consensus among meteorologists or geologists. In our century, psychologists, sociologists, political scientists, and many others have gone far to establish a basic understanding of human individual and social behavior.

The quality of the teaching of the social sciences in the primary and secondary schools is a scandal that no one denies. No young person with a zest and aptitude for science is likely to be attracted to those subjects by what he learns of them before he reaches college, or is likely even to perceive them as subjects to which the scientific method applies. Recruitment to the social sciences has been too much a story of born-again scientists, converted from their initial commitment to physics or chemistry or biology. If one of the goals of scientific literacy is to expose youth to the whole range of opportunities for careers of intellectual challenge and excitement, then that goal is poorly served by contemporary education in the social sciences.

And now I will reveal my own biases and identifications. I believe that answering the question of "What is mind?" is one of the most exciting and important directions of scientific inquiry today. I believe that this direction, usually labeled cognitive science, will make an important contribution to the definition of scientific literacy and to the discovery of the most effective means for working toward it — and perhaps also toward delimiting the boundaries of the attainable. In building a curriculum for scientific literacy, it will be important to sample cognitive science as one of its components, as well as computer science, upon which research in cognition now so heavily relies.

CONCLUSION

In my paper, I have presented the reasons why it is important, in our kind of society, for T. C. Mits to have more than a little acquaintance with science, technology, and mathematics, quite independently of his or her vocational needs. I have argued that these subjects are an essential part of liberal education and of education for citizenship.

With respect to citizenship education, the essential skill is the ability to manage the experts — to gain the advantages of their expertise without becoming dependent upon them or vulnerable to their biases and identifications. But it is illusory to suppose that this skill can be developed purely by training in the forensic arts, or in other subjects that are independent of science. For their adequate development, members of society require no little knowledge of science, and especially a genuine understanding of scientific method, grounded in concrete experience with that method.

In liberal education it is even less feasible to skirt the sciences and mathematics; for these subjects address directly and profoundly the questions of our place in the world that are most central to the goals of liberal learning.

The more importance we attach to universal education in the sciences, the more important it becomes to establish realistic and realizable goals. But we have only a slight understanding of the magnitude and origins of individual differences in the ability to assimilate scientific and mathematical skills and knowledge. And we have less understanding of the methods that will be effective in dealing with the illiteracy of those who evidence, or claim, or even boast of, incorrigibility. Gaining that understanding must be assigned high priority among the research goals of cognitive science.

And finally, all of the arguments for the essentiality of education in the sciences apply as strongly to the social and behavioral sciences as they do to the physical and biological sciences. It is as important that we understand ourselves as that we understand the matter of which we are made and the universe in which we live. At the present time, we do almost nothing at the pre-university level to satisfy T. C. Mits' need to understand psychological and social processes and structures. Meeting that need must be added to the agenda of science education.

Haydn and Eighteenth-Century Patronage in Austria and Hungary

H. C. ROBBINS LANDON

THE TANNER LECTURES ON HUMAN VALUES

Delivered at
Clare Hall, Cambridge University

February 25 and 26, 1983

H. C. ROBBINS LANDON was educated at Swarthmore College and Boston University. He founded the Haydn Society in Boston in 1949 and subsequently settled in Vienna, where he became a member of the Zentralinstitut für Mozartforschung (Salzburg), a contributor to the British Broadcasting Corporation, and a contributor to the Neue Mozart Ausgabe. He has held visiting professorships at Queen's College (New York) and the University of California, and, from 1971, was Honorary Professorial Fellow, University College Cardiff (South Wales). Since 1978 he has been John Bird Professor of Music, University College Cardiff.

Professor Landon's publications include critical editions of music by Leopold and Wolfgang Mozart and a number of others. In all, he has published 18,000 pages of Haydn in score. His books on Haydn include the collected correspondence and London notebooks as well as a five-volume biography. From 1945 on, he has published some two hundred articles in various journals, and since 1962 he has been editor of the Haydn Yearbook.

INTRODUCTION

Haydn is generally considered, and with some justification, to be the typical case of an eighteenth-century Capellmeister, responsible to a rich prince and kept in some kind of superior vassalage. While the first part of the description is valid, the second is based on a profound misunderstanding of the musicians' rôle in a princely court such as that of the Esterházys. Haydn was considered to have the rank of an army officer — not a surprising rôle at the Esterházy court if we consider that Prince Nicolaus (reigned 1762–1790) was a famous general and the Prince's second-in-command an army captain. In this survey, I try to describe Haydn's and the other musicians' position at the court (which lived for most of the year in Hungary); but, also, Haydn's gradual emancipation from that position, illustrating his change in status by his and his patron's letters, some recently discovered. Naturally, Haydn is of particular importance to Western music — and hence to Western civilization — and it is essential that we understand the circumstances in which his art flourished and during which he gained an international reputation.

In recent years we have become ever more fascinated and horrified by the fate of Mozart, whose earthly remains were buried in an anonymous grave outside the city walls of Vienna. That event, the indignity of which gradually became infamous, took place in 1791, not quite a decade before the eighteenth century came to an end. But Mozart's death — though particularly appalling in view of his special genius — was by no means unique. Thousands of more modest composers and performers were ignominiously buried, often in mass graves which became, as it were, anonymous overnight. A roll call chosen at random might include:

Antonio Vivaldi, once the astonishment of *settecento* Europe, died in abject poverty at Vienna in 1741. His grave is unknown, and for many years it was not even known that he had died in Austria.

Carlos d'Ordoñez, a then well-known composer of Austro-Spanish parents, died in penury at Vienna in 1786.

Carl Ditters von Dittersdorf, once the most popular composer of German-language operas, died at Neuhof in Bohemia in 1799, his desk drawer full of symphonies that no one wanted to perform or publish.

Anton Huberty, once a celebrated Parisian music publisher and string player, who had issued Haydn's first symphonies in Paris in the 1760s, died at Vienna in 1791. His effects were hardly enough to keep his daughters from starvation.[1]

Luigi Boccherini, the Italian composer once famous throughout Europe, died 'in dire poverty' at Madrid in 1805, his music no longer fashionable.

Balanced against such a list we must place Handel, who died at London in 1759, his bank account full and the walls of his Brook Street house covered with Rembrandts and paintings of other Dutch masters; or Arcangelo Corelli, who died at Rome in 1713, surrounded by the beautiful instruments and paintings of which he was a fastidious collector. He left to his great patron, Cardinal Pietro Ottoboni, a picture of his choice; and in Corelli's apartments was a 'real gallery', a Breugel that he left to Cardinal Colonna, a Madonna by Sassoferrato and another by Cignani: a total of 136 paintings or 'disegni', ranging from Lotti and Salva-

---

[1] Alexander Weinmann, *Beiträge zur Geschichte des Alt-Wiener Musikverlages*, 'Kataloge Anton Huberty (Wien) und Christoph Torricella' (Vienna 1962), p. 7.

tore Rosa to Poussin. And on the list of composers who died in comfortable circumstances, we should perhaps close with Joseph Haydn, who died in 1809 a moderately wealthy man.[2]

Of course, good or bad luck must have played a decisive rôle in many cases, but there is little doubt that the fates of a Handel, Corelli, or Haydn were less characteristic than those of a Mozart, Vivaldi, or Boccherini.

And in proceeding from the general to the particular, why the musicians of the Esterházy court? For one thing, the archives, which are in the process of being published in Cologne and Cardiff, are the most complete of their kind in Europe. We have nothing like this detailed record for the archiepiscopal court at Salzburg or the electoral court at Bonn, where Mozart and Beethoven, respectively, grew up; nor have we such detailed records for many large cities. We have no idea what Johann Peter Salomon paid his musicians when Haydn was in London, or what Beethoven earned from his first great benefit concert in the Hofburgtheater of Vienna in 1800. Hence the information from the Esterházy Archives, in its prodigious detail, is doubly welcome, not least because the Esterházys' musical establishment was directed by Haydn from May 1761 until his retirement at the end of 1803.

The Esterházy family emerged into prominence and wealth primarily as a result of the Austro-Turkish wars, in which — contrary to almost all the other Hungarian noble families — the Esterházys chose the Hapsburg side. When the Austrians pushed the Turks back from Vienna's city walls precisely three hundred years ago, the Esterházys were richly rewarded with castles, lands, sinecures, and positions. Moreover, the Esterházys married well, adding large estates through their wives. From counts they were created perpetual princes by Emperor Leopold I late in 1687.

By the time Haydn joined the family in 1761, the Esterházys had a small choir and orchestra resident primarily in Eisenstadt,

[2] Mario Rinaldi, *Arcangelo Corelli* (Milan 1953), pp. 258f., 344ff.

thirty miles from Vienna, in what was then (and was indeed until after World War I) Hungary. The Chief Capellmeister was the church composer Gregor Werner, who was then old and unwell, and was in fact to die five years later, in March 1766. Haydn was engaged by Prince Paul Anton, who was married to a Marchesa Lunati-Visconti, but the Prince was dead less than a year later — in March 1762. Paul Anton was succeeded by his younger brother Nicolaus, who was also passionately fond of music and himself an expert performer on the violoncello and baryton (a kind of viola da gamba).

Prince Nicolaus proved to be one of his family's greatest administrators, something for which his illustrious military career (in the course of which the Empress Maria Theresa had honoured him) no doubt well prepared him. He soon reorganized the administration into a kind of gigantic pyramid, with the upper point, after Nicolaus himself, filled by another military man, Captain Peter Ludwig von Rahier, who was Regent and Chief Administrator of the Esterházy estates. His was a position of tremendous power, and his salary was correspondingly large. As Estates Director, his duties were widespread and included the supervision and administration of all the vast Esterházy lands and their many peoples, which encompassed parts of present Austria, Poland, Russia, Yugoslavia, Roumania, Hungary, and Czechoslovakia. Rahier was undoubtedly a martinet, but he tried to be fair, and he certainly took immense pains to stamp out corruption. If he often appears to be harsh, leniency was not a characteristic of life in Hungary in those days, an age on which the mild rays of the Enlightenment had not yet shone.

The musicians occupied a position more elevated than is usually believed. They were so-called 'house officers', which meant in military, and thus Rahier's, language that they were considered as officers and in no way as servants. They dined at the officers' mess if they were single and wore a handsome uniform, one for winter and a lighter one for summer. The servants were divided into two classes, those who wore livrée and those of the lower orders (kitchen and stable personnel, gardeners' assistants, and so forth). Prince Esterházy had five male personal servants-in-waiting, four of the 'lower orders', two runners, two pages (one a Negro and one the father of the celebrated violinist Bridge-tower for whom Beethoven wrote the 'Kreutzer' Sonata), and a bodyguard.

When the musicians were engaged, they received a contract, usually in German but occasionally in French or Italian, if the musician were unable to read German. In April 1761, when the orchestra was being reorganized by Haydn and many new musicians engaged, they hired a new flautist, one Franz Sigl. His contract is typical:

1mo . . . [He is engaged as flautist and oboist] but he should rather turn to, and thus qualify in, the Houbois. [He] is to conduct himself soberly, modestly, quietly and honestly, and is to appear neatly, in white stockings, white linen, pow-dered, with either pigtail or hair-bag . . . ; 2do . . . He shall appear daily in the anti-chambre before and after mid-day, and after his orders have been received he shall appear promptly at the designated time; . . . 3^{tio} . . . said Frantz Sigl shall be required at the Herrschaft's table, there to await the orders of his Serene Princely Highness either during the meal to play music on any of those instruments on which he is skilled or, like the other house officers, not to shirk serving the Herrschaften; 4to The Fleutraversist shall be required to par-ticipate in the wind band at Eysenstadt, Kitsee, or in other places where the princely Grenadier Company mounts guard, exercises and parades, and likewise to play with the choir Musique at Eysenstadt. [Furthermore, he must follow the orders of the Ober- and Vice-Capel-Meister and submit peti-tions only through them.]; 5to Said Frantz Sigl shall not pro-duce any Musique at balls, theatrical representations or at other Herrschaften without special permission of the Prince, and 6to said Fleutraversist should acquit himself of such duties as are required of him as befits a worthy house officer; and just as the Serene Herrschaft does not consider it necessary to put on paper all those his duties, so they are graciously minded to hope that the said Frantz Sigl shall of his own free will observe his duties most exactly, and they rely on the ableness and honour of every man; 7mo [his salary shall be 20 gulden Rhenish monthly]; 8to [he shall receive a suit of clothes or uniform annually which he must look after]; 9mo [this contract is valid for one year from 1 April;] Given at Vienna, 1st April 1761.

The salary of twenty Rhenish gulden per month meant 240 gulden or florins per annum, which was considered good pay. When a few years later the musicians wanted to receive free medicine from the Hospitallers in Eisenstadt, an institution founded and supported by the Esterházy family, the Prince refused, saying that his musicians were sufficiently well paid not to have to receive free medicine.[3]

Married musicians did not eat at the officers' table but received a *Deputat*, or goods in kind. Everyone received wood and candles as well as free lodging, while families received in addition pork, beef, wheat, and so on, the precise quantity depending on the size of the family.

In 1761, when Haydn joined the court, all the members of the orchestra received 20 gulden per month except Haydn and Werner, who had 33 gulden 20 Kreuzer, and two violinists, Luigi Tomasini, the leader, and another musician, both of whom drew only 12 gulden 20 Kreuzer per month because they had been engaged as valets and were still paid according to that lower grade of employment.

When Haydn's younger brother, Johann Michael, was engaged by the Archbishop of Salzburg, Sigismund von Schrattenbach, in August 1763, Michael received 25 gulden monthly and a place at

---

[3] U. Tank, 'Die Dokumente der Esterházy-Archive zur fürstlichen Hofkapelle 1761–1770', *Haydn-Studien* IV:3–4 (1980), p. 206, and also *Haydn-Studien* III:2 (1974), p. 94. Before 1764, the musicians received free medicine, but now, writing from Vienna on 27 December 1764, Prince Nicolaus remarks 'but the other musicians [i.e., not Haydn] are sufficiently well paid anyway so that they can pay for their own medicines . . .'. Sigl's contract is in H. C. Robbins Landon, *Haydn Chronicle and Works; The Early Years, 1732–1765* (London: Thames and Hudson, and Bloomington: University of Indiana Press, 1980), p. 348.

the officers' table; and in 1763 this sum was also Leopold Mozart's salary as Vice-Capellmeister in Salzburg, whereby Leopold received neither meals at the officers' mess nor a *Deputat* (the goods in kind). Joseph Haydn, being married, received — apart from his summer and winter uniforms — the equivalent in kind of 182 gulden 30 Kreuzer per annum. Consequently, he was much better paid than Leopold Mozart with his family of two children.

In 1767, the Primas of Poland, Archbishop Prince Rodosky, engaged a group of musicians who were divided in two categories: the higher grade (e.g., horn players) received slightly less than seventeen gulden per month, the lower grade fourteen. Moreover, one clause in all the Polish contracts read: '2do Apart from their music, they are without fail to perform other duties appropriate to princely livrée, when the circumstances require it.' [4] In the Esterházy court, the musicians, being officers, were not expected to take on the duties of the liveried servants, which were in a different, lower class of employees, as we have just seen.

What could 240 gulden per annum purchase in 1761? A *Speckschwein* (fattened pig) cost six gulden, a *Frischling* (young wild boar or 'black pig') four gulden, an ox ten or twelve gulden, a milch cow eight. A fathom cord of wood cost three to four gulden. An inexpensive suit of clothes in Vienna cost seven gulden. In Eisenstadt, the local wine cost one-and-one-half to three Kreuzer for half a litre (sixty Kreuzer were one gulden), a pint of beer was two Kreuzer, a pound of beef, five-and-one-half Kreuzer, four eggs, one Kreuzer. Masons and carpenters earned twenty-seven Kreuzer daily. If he took his salary in kind, a mason could have four chickens, or one suckling pig and one chicken, or 108 eggs. Food, then, was cheap and plentiful.[5]

The principal problem was that of a pension. If a musician were seriously ill, the Prince often paid for the cure, but it was

---

[4] *Miscellanea Musicologia* VI. Svazek (Prague 1958), pp. 98f.
[5] Albert Riedl, "Halbvergessenes Eisenstadt', in *Eisenstadt. 300 Jahre Freistadt* (Eisenstadt 1948), p. 64; also Janos Harich in *Haydn Year Book* IV, 9f.

not customary to pay pensions to old musicians. There were exceptions for those who had been especially long at court or whom the Prince wished particularly to reward, but the conferring of a pension was still primarily an ex gratia gesture.

Case One: the princely contractor, called *Ingenieur*, Nicolaus Jacoby, had been in service since 1746 and had worked on Eszterháza Castle; he was pensioned after twenty-nine years of service on 1 January 1775, with a yearly income of 300 gulden, which was to pass undiminished to his widow and children, so long as any of them lived. In toto the Esterházy estate disbursed some 10,000 gulden each year in pensions.

Case Two: Widow Catherine Dietzl wrote a petition to Prince Nicolaus Esterházy in which she asked for a pension. Her husband, Joseph Dietzl Senior, had entered the princely service as a tenor in 1753. At the same time he had been created the castle schoolmaster and had played second violin in the church orchestra. It had, moreover, been his responsibility to submit the yearly expenses for the church music to the princely accounts officer. In 1773 he was to become organist. But in 1768, as a result of an internal reform, he had been threatened with expulsion from the church music. Since he could hardly live from his small salary as schoolmaster, Haydn asked the Prince to raise Dietzl's salary or to retain him in the church music (more of this later). As a result, Dietzl's dismissal was cancelled in 1769 and he was reinstated in the church choir until his death in 1777.

The widow pointed out that her late husband had been castle schoolmaster for twenty-six years, and that he had been ill for several years before his death; this lingering illness had involved costly medicines and doctors' bills. Now she was sunk in debt, her eyes so weak that she could not work, she had had twenty-four children and was now a pauper; she throws herself on Prince Nicolaus's mercy. The answer on the document was: *nihil.*[6]

---

[6] Acta Musicalia 40, Esterházy Archives, National Széchényi Library, Budapest, *Haydn Year Book* XIV (1984).

Among the musicians at the Esterházy court were also lower groups: first, the church musicians who remained at Eisenstadt when the court moved to Eszterháza. These church musicians received considerably less money than the secular musicians. But there was a third group, the copyists. Usually this position was very badly paid, which led to the following series of letters from an Esterházy copyist of the 1760s, Anton Adolph. He received his salary, as princely copyist, from the major domo's office at Eisenstadt along with the liveried servants. For this reason his name does not appear in any list of musicians. He is mentioned for the first time in 1762 in the major domo's office with a monthly salary of twelve gulden. In 1763, he addressed the following petition to the Prince:

To Your High-princely Serenity Prince Nicolaus, Prince of the Holy Roman Empire and Lord of Esterházy and Galanta, Count of Forchtenstein, etc. my high-commanding most gracious prince and lord, etc. Most Serene Prince of the Empire, General Field Marshal Lieutenant, High-commanding, most gracious prince and lord, May Your High-princely Serenity most graciously deign to consider that in the course of a year I have already copied about 1000 sheets of music and ruled them (without any remuneration) and worked most diligently.

Since I have no other means of income I request some high-condescending help at discretion as I am not able to pay from my monthly salary the rent of a house, wood, candles and other necessities.

So may my abject petition reach your High-princely Serenity to help me, poor as I am, in my utter distress.

Your High-princely Serenity's and my high-commanding, most gracious prince and lord's

Most obedient servant

Anton Adolph

Copyist[7]

---

[7] Acta Musicalia 14, ibid., in *Haydn Year Book* XIII (1982).

Since there was no reaction to this suggestion, at least on the document, we find another petition, which reads as follows:

Most Serene Highness and Noble Prince of the Holy Roman Empire, Gracious and Dread Lord!

It will be known to Your Serene Prince Highness in your infinite grace that I, a poor copyist, Antonji Adolph, have often submissively requested Your Princely Highness in your gracious mercy to improve my yearly salary; for I, a poor man, who is also married, have no more each month than twelve gulden in cash, together with the livery like other servants, and from this my meagre salary I must not only pay for my lodgings but also for wood, candles, and must support myself, miserably, even though I am crushed with work, so that as copyist I work day and night to supply the operas and comedies, as the enclosed bill will attest. And not only must I copy all this but even supply my own ink.

Considering that for all this I receive only 12 fl. and the livery (but without cost), it is difficult especially when it rains or snows, which is bad for the paper I take back and forth; that I have to pay for my lodgings, wood and especially candles because I have to write so much at night; that my yearly salary, which is anyway not large, is stretched to the utmost; therefore I beg Your Serene Princely Highness on my knees, in humility and submissiveness, that in your graciousness (known to the whole world) you grant me some improvement in my monthly salary, or something towards lodgings, wood or candles; for which act of grace God the Almighty will reward you richly, but I with my poor wife will pray to God every day in our prayers to grant rich blessings to Your Serene Princely Highness. And so I comfort myself that you will heed this my request, and remain, Your Serene Princely Highness's

Humble and Submissive Servant,
Antonji Adolph

SPECIFICATION

What was copied for Your Serene Princely Highness for operas and comedies [he means German-language operettas], paper lined and copied, from 3 May to the month of August this year 1763, viz. [There follows a list of 832 sheets, one bifolium equalling four pages, or a total of 3,328 pages. The list is, incidentally, of vital importance to us because it identifies and dates Symphony No. 72, hitherto undated and obviously in wrong chronological position; it should be forty numbers earlier.]

This petition fell on deaf ears, and Adolph ran away from Eisenstadt the next year and was never heard of again. His successor was Joseph Elssler, who in 1769 also petitioned the Prince for a raise in salary:

[Prince Nicolaus's titles omitted here]

Serene high-born Prince of the Empire,

Most gracious and high-commanding Lord and Master

It is hard for me to trouble Your Serene Highness with my requests, but to whom shall I have recourse unless to my best, most indulgent and most gracious Prince who so willingly helps the needy and will not, therefore, close his generous heart to my most submissive request?

I have a wife and four children and as my monthly salary of twelve florins [gulden] will no longer cover our expenses, my most humble and submissive request is submitted to Your Serene Highness for the gracious allowance of some increase of pay as shall be seen fit; for which great favour God will be the rich recompense.

In the hope of a favourable hearing I remain with the profoundest respect and humility, falling at the feet of Your Serene Highness,

Joseph Elssler   Copyist.[8]

Elssler did not succeed in causing the standard salary of twelve gulden per month to be raised, but in his case, Haydn, who acted as a diplomat and buffer between his musicians and the court administration, was able to assist by engaging Joseph Elssler as his personal

[8] Acta Musicalia 11, in *Haydn Year Book* XIII (1982).

copyist. Music sent abroad, that is not on official Esterházy business, was copied by Elssler and the copying charges paid by Haydn. Many of these copies survive and are of the utmost importance textually.

After Elssler's death in 1782 a new system for the princely copyist was introduced. (Actually the new copyist was engaged in 1780, when Elssler was presumably unable to cope with all the increased copying work engendered by the regular operatic season now being given at Eszterháza Castle.) Instead of receiving a blanket salary, the new princely copyist, Johann Schellinger, was paid by the page; but he also received a small salary as the official prompter. His task was a crushing one: in 1786, Schellinger copied 1,719 bifolium sheets of vocal parts at seven Kreuzer per Bogen or bifolium sheet, and 1,817 sheets of instrumental parts at five Kreuzer per Bogen, a staggering total of 14,264 pages. Haydn countersigned this incredible bill on 29 December 1786. For this copying work Schellinger was paid at the going rate in Vienna: a total of 335 gulden 28 Kreuzer. In that same year, 1786, Johann Schellinger petitioned the Prince for help. '. . . through no fault of mine I have had to endure a grave illness, as Your Highness knows', writes the copyist. He asks the Prince to take over the expenses of the illness, 'for my whole monthly salary has had to go for the baths, food and small things'. Schellinger presented the bills in the amount of 32 gulden 10 Kreuzer. 'It is hard for me to pay it all'. Prince Nicolaus promptly paid the bill.[9]

In a court that employed Haydn, our interest must of course centre on the composer himself. The documents in the Esterházy Archives tell their own story of Haydn's diplomatic and musical success. In a series of receipts which have just been discovered, we learn an interesting fact. When Haydn was engaged by Prince Paul Anton in 1761, the composer's salary was 400 gulden. The

---

[9] H. C. Robbins Landon, *Haydn Chronicle and Works; Haydn at Eszterháza, 1766–1790* (London: Thames and Hudson, and Bloomington: University of Indiana Press, 1978), pp. 679–82, with the appropriate references for the original German.

Capellmeister, Haydn's director, also earned that sum. Now the new documents show Haydn being paid a secret additional salary from the princely privy purse, the first dated 31 October 1761 for fifty gulden 'additional salary' for the quarter 1 August–31 October. In other words, Haydn received apart from his stated salary of 400 gulden another secret 200 gulden. This 600 gulden is the official salary that he received after Prince Nicolaus succeeded his brother in April 1762. The new sum is recorded in a princely decree of 25 June 1762. It is now considered likely that this whole operation was initiated by Prince Paul Anton so as not to offend Capellmeister Werner, who was to remain in ignorance that his assistant was receiving one third more salary than he. Perhaps Prince Nicolaus saw no reason to continue the deception.[10] The official recognition of all this no doubt materially increased Werner's famous jealousy of Haydn which culminated in the well-known protest about him that Werner sent to the Prince in the autumn of 1765.

At the beginning, Haydn's position *vis-à-vis* Prince Nicolaus was one of a certain stiffness. The Regent, Rahier, was as we have said a harsh taskmaster. Haydn protested about Rahier to the Prince in 1765, writing that 'We could not get anywhere with the Regent, and I even had to put up with his slamming the door in my face. . . . Your Serene and Illustrious Highness must yourself remember in your graciousness that I cannot serve two masters, and cannot accept the commands of, and subordinate myself to, the Regent; for Your Serene and Illustrious Highness once said to me, "Come first to me, because I am his master".' [11]

In the ensuing years we see again and again Haydn intervening for musicians threatened with dismissal, or punishment, or fines for supposed misdemeanours. In most instances Haydn was

---

[10] See Tank, 'Die Dokumente der Esterházy-Archive', *Haydn-Studien* IV, p. 163 (document 31).

[11] Landon, *The Early Years*, pp. 413f., with appropriate references to the source for the German original.

successful — not always, but there were to be increasing numbers of cases where the original decision was reversed. Nevertheless, in these years Haydn always preferred to use a go-between in his dealings with the autocratic and melancholy Prince. In the 1760s the go-between was Anton Scheffstoss, whose daughter married the principal 'cellist Joseph Weigl. In one instance we have a letter to the Prince which Haydn wrote out twice, the first time as a draft for Scheffstoss to approve:

> In case you find anything imprudent in the above [letter] let me know of it at once. I flatter myself that through my petition and through your confirmation of it, something may have an effect on His Highness. Apart from wishing you best greetings for the coming Holidays, and a happy farewell to the old and welcome to the new year, I am, Highly respected Sir,
>
> Your obedient servant,
Joseph Haydn manu propria.
>
> Eisenstadt, 22nd December 1768.[12]

The petition was to prevent the dismissal of two musicians who also fulfilled other duties: Rent Collector Franz Nigst, leader of the second violins in the main orchestra, and Joseph Dietzl of the church choir, whose widow, as we have seen, had petitioned unsuccessfully for a pension after his death. Haydn's intervention was successful on both counts.

Later, as Prince Nicolaus grew old, letters of this kind grew rarer and finally ceased altogether. Haydn was, in the 1780s, on sufficiently easy terms with his Prince to accomplish most of his wishes through personal interviews. In the 1760s, Prince Nicolaus liked to reward the musicians and especially Haydn with presents of gold coins — a welcome addition to the usual salaries. Haydn's own salary gradually rose so that by 1775 it and the emoluments amounted to 961 gulden 45 Kreuzer, the third highest salary of the entire Esterházy court, surpassed only by those of the Regent

---

[12] Landon, *Haydn at Eszterháza*, p. 153.

and the physician in ordinary. When Prince Nicolaus died in 1790, he left Haydn the noble pension of 1000 gulden per annum. Mozart was then receiving 800 gulden from the Viennese court as Chamber Composer.

At the beginning of Haydn's career with the Esterházys, the composer knelt and kissed the hem of the Prince's coat in thanks for favours received: this was then standard practice on the Continent. Now, in 1790, a new prince Esterházy, Anton, succeeded to the title. He dismissed the very expensive opera troupe and the orchestra, retaining later only a wind band for the hunt and for *Tafelmusik*. Haydn was now free to travel and left for England, summoned by the great violinist and impresario Johann Peter Salomon.

As soon as Haydn arrived in London, he considered it polite to write at once to Prince Anton, who was still his employer although he was on a leave of absence:

Most noble Prince of the Holy Roman Empire!
I report respectfully that, despite unpleasant weather and a great many bad roads throughout the whole trip, I arrived in London this 2nd of January, happy and in good health. My arrival caused a great stir, and forced me to take larger quarters that same evening: I received so many calls that I shall hardly be able to repay them in six weeks. Both the ambassadors, i.e. Prince Castelcicala of Naples and Herr Baron von Stadion [called]; and I had the pleasure of lunching with both of them at 6 o'clock in the evening. The new opera libretto which I am to compose is entitled *Orfeo*. . . . [Haydn goes on to give details of the cast.] The concerts will begin next month on the 11th of February, and I shall dutifully write Your Highness more about that later. . . . I take the liberty of respectfully kissing the hands of the loveliest Princess, Your Highness's most charming wife, and also the Princess Marie and Her Highness's husband . . . '.[13]

13 Landon, *Haydn Chronicle and Works; Haydn in England, 1791–1795* (London: Thames and Hudson, and Bloomington: University of Indiana Press, 1976), p. 38.

It was not known hitherto if Prince Esterházy answered this letter, but now a whole further correspondence between Prince Anton and Haydn has come to light in the Esterházy Archives in Budapest, including the following revealing reply to Haydn's letter:

> Well and nobly born, much respected Herr Kapellmeister. With great pleasure I have received your letter of 8th January and the news contained therein that you arrived safely in London on the 2nd, and were so well received. I share most heartily in all this news and also in your future plans, not only about the opera which you are in the process of composing but all the other projects of which you inform me. I remain with great respect,
>
> Your most willing
Anton Prince Esterházy.
> Vienna, 3rd February 1791.

And several months later, after Haydn had reported on the astonishing success of his first London season, Prince Anton wrote from Eisenstadt in August 1791, 'With great pleasure I see from your letter of 20th July how very much your talents are appreciated in London, and I most heartily share in your success . . .'.[14]

From kissing the hem of a princely coat to this tone of correspondence was perhaps the most astonishing personal feat of Haydn's career, and one which he conducted so modestly and quietly that the effect is easily underestimated. Within a few years, after Haydn returned to Austria, we will find him dining at the Esterházys' high dinner table, the composer's health proposed by the Austrian Ambassador to St. James.[15] It is the record of a firm but unobtrusive social revolution, and one accomplished single-handedly.

---

[14] U. Tank, *Studien zur Esterhazyschen Hofmusik von etwa 1620 bis 1790* (Regensburg 1981), pp. 285f.

[15] Landon, *Haydn Chronicle and Works; The Late Years, 1801–1809* (London: Thames and Hudson, and Bloomington: University of Indiana Press, 1979), p. 231.

EDITOR'S NOTE. H. C. Robbins Landon's Tanner Lectures were the first to feature a musical performance as part of the proceedings. The following information was provided by Lord Ashby of Clare Hall, University of Cambridge:

It was not possible to cover the entire content of these lectures in the printed record. The first lecture, reproduced here, was the preamble to a second lecture in which Professor Landon discussed the practicalities of writing for the musicians and instruments of the day, as well as the influence of music upon eighteenth-century thought. During the lecture, the Academy of Ancient Music demonstrated the use made of baroque instruments in Haydn's day. The next day a concert of Haydn's music was given by the Academy under the direction of Christopher Hogwood, using baroque instruments to illustrate points made in the two lectures.

The seminar that followed the lectures brought together scholars of music, conductors, music critics, editors of music journals, performers from the Academy of Ancient Music, makers of musical instruments, and a picked group of students, to discuss the significance of music in eighteenth-century society.

In association with the lectures, an exhibition of instruments from Haydn's time was mounted in the music school. The exhibition emphasized the immense amount of information on Viennese instrument makers which exists in the Esterházy archives and which has been made available through Professor Landon's publications.

THE TANNER LECTURERS

1976–77

OXFORD
Bernard Williams, Cambridge University

MICHIGAN
Joel Feinberg, University of Arizona
"Voluntary Euthanasia and the Inalienable Right to Life"

STANFORD
Joel Feinberg, University of Arizona
"Voluntary Euthanasia and the Inalienable Right to Life"

1977–78

OXFORD
John Rawls, Harvard University

MICHIGAN
Sir Karl Popper, University of London
"Three Worlds"

STANFORD
Thomas Nagel, Princeton University

1978–79

OXFORD
Thomas Nagel, Princeton University
"The Limits of Objectivity"

CAMBRIDGE
C. C. O'Brien, London

MICHIGAN
Edward O. Wilson, Harvard University
"Comparative Social Theory"

STANFORD
Amartya Sen, Oxford University
"Equality of What?"

UTAH
Lord Ashby, Cambridge University
"The Search for an Environmental Ethic"

UTAH STATE
R. M. Hare, Oxford University
"Moral Conflicts"

1979–80

OXFORD
Jonathan Bennett, Univ. of British Columbia
"Morality and Consequences"

CAMBRIDGE
Raymond Aron, Collège de France
"Arms Control and Peace Research"

HARVARD
George Stigler, University of Chicago
"Economics or Ethics?"

MICHIGAN   Robert Coles, Harvard University
                "Children as Moral Observers"

STANFORD   Michel Foucault, Collège de France
                "Omnes et Singulatim: Towards a Criticism
                of 'Political Reason' "

UTAH   Wallace Stegner, Los Altos Hills, California
                "The Twilight of Self-Reliance: Frontier Values
                and Contemporary America"

1980–81

OXFORD   Saul Bellow, University of Chicago
                "A Writer from Chicago"

CAMBRIDGE   John A. Passmore, Australian National University
                "The Representative Arts as a Source of Truth"

HARVARD   Brian M. Barry, University of Chicago
                "Do Countries Have Moral Obligations? The Case
                of World Poverty"

MICHIGAN   John Rawls, Harvard University
                "The Basic Liberties and Their Priority"

STANFORD   Charles Fried, Harvard University
                "Is Liberty Possible?"

UTAH   Joan Robinson, Cambridge University
                "The Arms Race"

HEBREW UNIV.   Solomon H. Snyder, Johns Hopkins University
                "Drugs and the Brain and Society"

1981–82

OXFORD   Freeman Dyson, Princeton University
                "Bombs and Poetry"

CAMBRIDGE   Kingman Brewster, President Emeritus, Yale University
                "The Voluntary Society"

HARVARD   Murray Gell-Mann, California Institute of Technology
                "The Head and the Heart in Policy Studies"

MICHIGAN   Thomas C. Schelling, Harvard University
                "Ethics, Law, and the Exercise of Self-Command"

STANFORD   Alan A. Stone, Harvard University
                "Psychiatry and Morality"

UTAH	R. C. Lewontin, Harvard University
	"Biological Determinism"
AUSTRALIAN	
NATL. UNIV.	Leszek Kolakowski, Oxford University
	"The Death of Utopia Reconsidered"

1982–83

OXFORD	Kenneth J. Arrow, Stanford University
	"The Welfare-Relevant Boundaries of the Individual"
CAMBRIDGE	H. C. Robbins Landon, University College, Cardiff
	"Haydn and Eighteenth-Century Patronage in Austria and Hungary"
HARVARD	Bernard Williams, Cambridge University
	"Morality and Social Justice"
STANFORD	David Gauthier, University of Pittsburgh
	"The Incompleat Egoist"
UTAH	Carlos Fuentes, Princeton University
	"A Writer from Mexico"
JAWAHARLAL	
NEHRU UNIV.	Ilya Prigogine, University of Brussels
	"Only an Illusion"

1983–84

OXFORD	Donald D. Brown, Carnegie Institution of Washington, Baltimore
CAMBRIDGE	Stephen J. Gould, Harvard University
	"Evolutionary Hopes and Realities"
HARVARD	Kenneth J. Arrow, Stanford University
MICHIGAN	Herbert A. Simon, Carnegie-Mellon University
	"Scientific Literacy as a Goal in a High-Technology Society"
STANFORD	Leonard B. Meyer, University of Pennsylvania
	"Ideology and Music in the Nineteenth Century"
UTAH	Helmut Schmidt, former Chancellor, West Germany
	"The Future of the Atlantic Alliance"
HELSINKI	Georg Henrik von Wright, Helsinki
	"Of Human Freedom"

General Indices

THE TANNER LECTURES ON HUMAN VALUES

VOLUMES I–V

INDEX TO VOLUME I, 1980
THE TANNER LECTURES ON HUMAN VALUES

A

Abortion, 231

Abstract objects. *See* world 3, abstract objects in; abstract thought content in

Abstraction, 83, 85

Act-utilitarianism, 180–82

Adams, Samuel, on rights, 246, 256–57

Advantage utility, 204, 215

Aesthetics, 107; problems of, 150

Agent-neutral: defined, 102. *See also* reasons, agent-neutral; values, agent neutral

Agent-relative: defined, 102. *See also* reasons, agent-relative; values, agent-relative

Altruism, 9–10, 12; "as if," 14; genuine, 13; kin-, 21; vs. self-interest, 12–13

Amorality, 137

Anthropocentrism, 53

Anthropology, 53, 55

Appearance: as a medium, 86; and perspective, 78; and reality, 115; vs. reality, 100, 113, 115; as subjective, 77, 98

Aquinas, St. Thomas, on suicide, 253

Aristotle, 174, 184, 252–53

Art, 151; dualistic view of, 150; monistic view of, 150; objective vs. subjective view of, 149–50; rejection of expressionist theory of, 152

Artificial intelligence, 165

Autocracy, 15

Autonomy, 120–21, 125–26, 256–57; as essential, 139; and rights of others, 252; subjective, 131; viewed objectively, 137

B

Badness: defined, 137

Basic capabilities, index of, 220

Basic capability equality, 197, 217, 220; criticism of, 219; defined, 218; as extension of Rawlsian equality, 219

Bedau, Hugo, on right to life, 224, 232

Beethoven's Fifth Symphony, 145, 148; dualistic view of, 147; monistic view of, 146–47

Behavior, 69; as distribution function, 53, 55–56, 66; genetically coded, 9–11, 22, 46; modification of attitudes toward sexual, 69; socially coded, 9–11, 46

Beliefs, 77; formed by objective standpoint, 115; as source of values, 98; as world 2 object, 160

Bentham, Jeremy, on utilitarianism, 192

Berkeley, George, on conceivability, 113

Berlin, Isaiah, on liberty, 238

Biogram: defined, 64

Blackstone, William, on rights, 243

Bradford, William, on wilderness, 26

Brain processes, 156, 160, 166; as world 1 object, 155

Bramah, Joseph, as inventor, 19

Burke, Edmund, on political and military plans, 163

C

Capital punishment, 225–26, 228, 231, 234, 244

Carter, Jimmy (President), on energy crisis, 46

Cartesian first person, 93

Case-implication: critique of, 197; perspective of, 201, 203–4, 208, 217

INDEX TO VOLUME II, 1981

THE TANNER LECTURES ON HUMAN VALUES

INDEX TO VOLUME IV, 1983
THE TANNER LECTURES ON HUMAN VALUES

[209]

INDEX TO VOLUME V, 1984

THE TANNER LECTURES ON HUMAN VALUES

A

Abelard, Pierre, 26

Actor-relative value: and egoism, 73, 75, 77, 113; as inconsistent, 77; maximization of, 72, 79–80, 92, 95, 97–99, 103, 106–7, 110; and rational choice strategies, 82; and rational morality, 94, 101; of reasons, 74–75

Adolph, Anton (copyist), 165–67

Analysis, vs. intuition, 135–36

Argentina: compared with Mexico, 15; history and culture of, 13; literature of, 14; today, 16; and use of Spanish language, 17

Arreola, Juan José, 31

Austen, Jane, 18

Austro-Turkish wars, 159

B

BASIC (computer language), 141

Baier, Kurt, on morality, 93–94

Bakhtin, Mikhail, 30

Balzac, Honoré de, 23, 30–31

Bargaining: in game theory, 116; as link between moral theory and theory of rational choice, 117–18

Beethoven, Ludwig von, 159, 161

Bergson, Henri, 41

Berliner, Hans, 8

Besso, Michele: death of, 38; on time, 37

Best response: defined, 81; of egoists, 92–93, 104, 106; example of, 91; and group choice, 102–4; and Prisoners' Dilemma, 98

Bifurcation: of chemical systems, 48–50; and symmetry, 53

Biology, and evolution, 42, 45

Boccherini, Luigi, 158–59

Bodet, Jaime Torres, 15

Bohr, Niels, on reality, 37

Boltzmann, Ludwig, 47–48, 51–52, 54, 58; on entropy increase, 43–44

Bonn, electoral court at, 159

Borges, Jorge Luis, 14, 17–18, 21

Brain, the: hemispheres of, 133–35; specialization of, 134

Brezhnev, Leonid, 11

Broch, Hermann, 6

Bruno, Giordano, 47; on the universe, 38–39

Buendía, Colonel, 3

Buñuel, Luis, 22

C

Caesar, Julius, 26

Camus, Albert, 24–25

Cané, 14

Canning, George, 11

Cárdenas, Lázaro, 7–9

Castillo, President, 13

Cervantes, Miguel de, 12, 25, 27, 31, 33

Chardin, Teilhard de, 41

Chemical clocks, as examples of equilibrium, 48

Chemistry: and irreversibility, 43; reconceptualization of, 57

Chile, history and literature of, 10–12

Choice: agents of, 70; collective, 102–4; egoistic, 105; and maximizing principle, 111

Choice set, defined, 81

Classical reason, nontemporal vision of, 41

THE TANNER LECTURES ON HUMAN VALUES, Volume V,
was composed in Intertype Garamond with Garamond Foundry display type
by Donald M. Henriksen, Scholarly Typography, Salt Lake City.